Contemplative Crochet

A Hands-On Guide for Interlocking Faith & Craft

Cindy Crandall-Frazier

Foreword by Linda Skolnik

Walking Together, Finding the Way ®
SKYLIGHT PATHS®
PUBLISHING
Woodstock, Vermont

Contemplative Crochet:
A Hands-On Guide for Interlocking Faith and Craft

2010 Quality Paperback Edition, Second Printing
2008 Quality Paperback Edition, First Printing
© 2008 by Cindy Crandall-Frazier

For information regarding permission to reprint material from this book, please mail or fax your request in writing to SkyLight Paths Publishing, Permissions Department, at the address / fax number listed below, or e-mail your request to permissions@skylightpaths.com

Grateful acknowledgment is given for permission to use the following material: Page 77, "Sun Birthing (Stages of the birth of a new sun)," by Xenobia Bailey, © Xenobia Bailey. Photograph by James Dee. Used by permission. Page 79, Mexican Mandala Necklace by Melody MacDuffee, © Melody MacDuffee. Used by permission. Page 108, "Tree Cozy" by Carol Hummel, © Carol Hummel. Used by permission.

Library of Congress Cataloging-in-Publication Data
Crandall-Frazier, Cindy, 1952–
Contemplative crochet : a hands-on guide for interlocking faith and craft / Cindy Crandall-Frazier.
p. cm.
Includes bibliographical references and index.
ISBN-13: 978-1-59473-238-6 (quality pbk.)
ISBN-10: 1-59473-238-8 (quality pbk.)
1. Knitting—Philosophy. 2. Spirituality. I. Title.
TT820.C8564 2008
746.43'2—dc22
2008031584

10 9 8 7 6 5 4 3 2

Manufactured in the United States of America
Cover Design: Jenny Buono
Photographs of *Contemplative Crochet* projects by Richard Frazier.
Photographs for project instructions by Valerie Broucek (www.valeriebroucek.com).
Crocheted samples for project instructions by Jane Brown, Craftique/Never Enough Knitting (www.craftique-neverenoughknitting.com).

SkyLight Paths Publishing is creating a place where people of different spiritual traditions come together for challenge and inspiration, a place where we can help each other understand the mystery that lies at the heart of our existence.

SkyLight Paths sees both believers and seekers as a community that increasingly transcends traditional boundaries of religion and denomination—people wanting to learn from each other, *walking together, finding the way.*

SkyLight Paths, "Walking Together, Finding the Way," and colophon are trademarks of LongHill Partners, Inc., registered in the U.S. Patent and Trademark Office.

Walking Together, Finding the Way®
Published by SkyLight Paths Publishing
A Division of Longhill Partners, Inc.
Sunset Farm Offices, Route 4, P.O. Box 237
Woodstock, VT 05091
Tel: (802) 457-4000   Fax: (802) 457-4004
www.skylightpaths.com

Two life-changing events accompanied the writing of this book:

My kindred spirit, Eleanor, died,

and two months later my first grandchild, Liam, was born.

This book is dedicated to both of them.

What happens in meditation is what happens in our acts of creativity: We become united with the Divine Spirit, which is the Spirit of Creation and Creativity. Our sixth chakras become dwelling places for the Divine. We con-temple there, that is, we share a sacred temple with the Divine. We call it "contemplation" or unity or forgetfulness of separation and duality. And then creativity surely flows.

—**MATTHEW FOX,** *Creativity:*
Where the Divine and the Human Meet

Contents

Index of Projects

Foreword

A classic book on creating dolls from socks was my first introduction to Cindy Crandall-Frazier. Her book *Sock Doll Workshop* shows anyone who can thread a needle how to make a beloved plaything. Although sewing was technically out of the purview of Patternworks, my knitting supply catalog, I felt the book would be as empowering and captivating to my customers as it was to me. And so my relationship with Cindy began.

It turned out that Cindy had a passion for crochet. I asked what about the hook spoke to her (as knitting needles spoke to me). The answer came in a short essay called "Why I Crochet," written in her characteristically thoughtful and thorough style. I've learned to trust and admire the quality, integrity, and originality of Cindy's work. Years after selling Patternworks, an exceptionally skilled knitting friend asked me how to get the pattern for Cindy's Community Crochet Adult Earflap Hat, which struck her as the essential warm hat—high praise, indeed, coming from this knitter.

What makes a particular pattern or book so compelling? The answer is contained in *Contemplative Crochet: A Hands-On Guide for Interlocking Faith and Craft.* Cindy invites readers to join her in tapping into "that vein of wealth that ties us to a vastly creative universe" and provides a cornucopia of inspiration, encouragement, tips, and nourishment for the way. It is a quest for finding the spiritual dimension in the rhythms of our lives.

At my weekly knitting group, my friends joined me in crocheting the book's Friends and Tea Cozy project, since we are kindred souls—already in and into the loop. Karen had been knitting a tea cozy the previous week and mentioned that knitting the beautiful corrugation was grueling work. This crochet pattern, however, provided the desired highly textured (and thermal) fabric. This change in craft knocked us out of the usual dynamic of the group. We worked as a team, helping one another along, and, actually—for the first time in our history—had long periods of silence. Wow! We laughed, some of us struggled, some fudged, and Cindy's instruction that "this pattern is forgiving" became our chorus. She was right. I'm looking forward to see what new paths open for our group as a result of this experience.

Contemplative Crochet was obviously a labor of love, written from the point of view of a wise and joyful woman who understands the wisdom of "just enough" and who can articulate what is close to her heart. I know it did me good to read this book, and I'll be coming back to it again.

LINDA SKOLNIK

Introduction

With hook in hand, I pause to contemplate the connections of my spirit to my hands, my hands to my craft. I am only one person at only one point on a never-ending continuum. As you join me, each of you will be starting in a different place. You may be new to crochet or a veteran crocheter. You may have picked up this book because you already sense a link between the quieting rhythm of crochet and the contemplative quality of spiritual seeking. You may have been reared in a spiritual setting or you may have chosen a spiritual home for yourself as you grew in your understanding of the Divine. Maybe you are a lifelong member of your chosen faith community but are looking for a way to personalize and deepen your spiritual life. Or perhaps you do not feel comfortable with formalized spiritual ideas, but seek a centering practice that will enrich your faith.

I learned my first spiritual lessons in a little white Methodist Church in a small town in upstate New York. One of the Sunday school stories that touched me most was the story of the good Samaritan, in which one person went out of his way—both personally and culturally—to help a stranger in need. I got it. This lesson of radical acceptance and radical love would eventually lead me away from my childhood church and on to a new spiritual adventure.

When my young friend Dolly invited me to attend meeting (a general term for Quaker worship gatherings) with her and her family, I was introduced to meditative silence as worship. In a Quaker meeting, the silence is broken only by the occasional person speaking a carefully listened for spiritual message. When I started to crochet, I realized that the meditative rhythm of crochet felt akin to attending a silent meeting.

Since childhood, I have been drawn to handwork of all kinds, especially to fiber and the fiber arts. In crochet, I found a range of philosophical and spiritual ties that fit together well for me. I especially value the intimacy of yarn and hands, and I marvel at being able to create beauty or to compassionately warm another person.

I have chosen a contemplative faith community. I have chosen a contemplative craft. In *Contemplative Crochet*, I have gathered a workbasket full of information, stories, and musings that have come from many corners of my life and link crochet and spiritual life in diverse ways. As you read, you will find phrases and ideas that have come from my life as a Quaker, as well as lessons that crochet itself has taught me.

I write from the perspective that everything we do is sacred, as long as it is done mindfully, inviting the Sacred into it. Each chapter concludes with a crochet project, some of which serve as simple reminders of a spiritual concept, others as actual tools to incorporate contemplation into your crochet practice.

Chapter 1, "Roots and Wings," is an exploration of what keeps our feet on the ground and what lifts us above the everyday mundane. My crochet beginnings, coupled with some background information about the craft of crochet, set the stage for the discovery of mystery that is sandwiched between the humdrum qualities of daily life and the joyful flight of creative activity. At the close of the chapter, the Roots and Wings Paperweight project, with a lacy crocheted top, serves a reminder that we need to stay grounded and to know joy.

Chapter 2 turns to the subject of "Plenty." What is it that makes us feel as though we have enough, more than enough? What shifts our perspective of what plenty is? What responsibilities come with our possession of plenty? I explore these ideas through Native

American, biblical, and mythological stories, along with an original tale. You will have an opportunity to create a small yarn cornucopia to sit on your desk or give as a gift to a yarn friend, as a symbol of plenty.

Moving from plenty to the other end of the continuum, chapter 3 embraces the idea that "The Power of Limits" can be a foundation for a richer experience. Where might prioritizing, focus, and order take us that chaos can't? How do we find those things in our lives? You will learn about a mathematical concept of limitation called "the golden proportion," which can be applied directly to crochet to give it visual power. This links to the shape of a pentagon, which is also the shape of morning glories. You will be able to make a Morning Glory Motif to remind yourself of the value of limits.

Chapter 4, "Meditation Meets Prayer," moves to the core benefits of crochet as a spiritual practice. Crochet is a fine vehicle with which to center yourself, connect with the Divine, and find peace. I have included not only some basic ideas for a simple meditation practice, but also some thoughts on the benefits of meditating with your crochet. You'll meet some members of a prayer shawl group and have an opportunity to crochet a prayer shawl to wrap yourself in for your devotional time, or to give as a gift.

The theme of meditation continues in chapter 5, "Circles and Cycles," which focuses on the art, meaning, and use of mandalas. I love mandalas for their artistic beauty, and I am fascinated with their religious uses and cultural ties. I explore mandalas as healing tools and then introduce you to some amazing crochet artists: two women who make crocheted mandalas and one who makes mandala-like forms into jewelry. The chapter concludes with instructions on how to make a portable crocheted mandala for your own meditation.

In chapter 6, "Prayers on a String," beads and crochet come together in another beautiful expression of crochet as a spiritual practice. I explore the use of prayer beads in many faith traditions and how they keep spiritual practice close at hand. You'll have the opportunity to crochet your own strand of prayer beads to wear around your neck.

"Pathfinding"—spiritual, vocational, and craft—is the subject of chapter 7. I touch on how George Fox, the founder of Quakerism, found his way through a forest of unanswered questions, and I include my own story of pathfinding in the hope that it might help you as you seek your way. Drawing on the meditative benefits of walking, I suggest ways to incorporate both meditation and movement into creative crochet work. At the end of this chapter, you will find the instructions for a "Way Opens" Scarf, which symbolizes how generous the universe can be when we are ready for and open to its gifts.

Crochet practice naturally shifts from contemplation into action in chapter 8, "From Heart to Hand." I hope you will enjoy meeting my knitting friends as I teach them how to crochet and my kindergarteners as they create colorful playthings out of crocheted chains. I also explore ways of teaching our craft and giving our crochet projects to others. As we become a link in the chain of teachers who help students, and our students in turn become teachers, we join in an ongoing crochet foundation that stretches into the future. We can also share the work of our hands, giving away our creations of comfort and love to people in need. I have included information about charitable organizations where crocheted materials are particularly welcome. A Friends and Tea Cozy project completes this chapter, with the suggestion that you gather a few friends and share your crocheting while indulging in the warmth of tea.

The last two chapters embrace subjects that are very dear to my heart. In "The Creative Spirit," chapter 9, I explore how creativity relates to us as crocheters, and how creativity relates us to our Creator. Then I turn to creative crochet in different cultural contexts and offer some suggestions to free your own creativity. You will also find a few tips for giving your creative work the emotional support that we all need at times. The chapter concludes with a free-form crochet project, a Scrumbled Tea Steeper, which will allow you to play with your crochet in an intuitive way.

The concluding chapter celebrates our hands, those extraordinary tools with which we wield all other tools. "The Blessings of Hands" begins with some simple physiology of hands and the early development of our crochet skills-to-be. I have also included a short section about two educational methods, Montessori and Waldorf, that revere children's hands, with Waldorf in particular using handwork as a complement to other subjects. Then I turn to religious traditions in which hand gestures play a central role as expressions of reverence, blessing, and petition. Chapter 10 also offers ways to "listen" to your hands and to tend them with exercises and massages when they are tired. At the conclusion of the chapter, you will find directions to make Lovingkindness Wristers as a caring way to tend your hands and wrists.

The projects in this book assume that you know the three basic stitches: single crochet, half double crochet, and double crochet, along with a few other basic skills, such as making a starting chain, using a slip stitch, and threading in ends. (If you need some help with basics, my book *Single Crochet for Beginners* offers many helpful instructions and photographs.) None of the projects in *Contemplative Crochet* are difficult if you follow the instructions. Some projects might hold a little challenge if you have only worked squares and rectangles with no stitch pattern and no shaping, but all are easy and rhythmic. Just jump in and try. Don't berate yourself if you need to try one a second time, or a third. Pat yourself on the back for developing your crochet skills and try again. Every worthwhile craft requires some patience. I have made some extra notes where I thought they would be helpful to carry you along.

At the close of each chapter I have included "queries." Queries are used in Quaker meetings to encourage deeper thinking and listening for the Spirit. These queries may be used to foster personal understanding or they may be used as discussion starters for groups. When Quakers work with queries, we try to allow silent spaces between responses. Then each person who wishes to speak expresses a complete idea without being interrupted by another. The short silence following each speaker contributes to a thoughtful and respectful tone. Whether you use the queries in this book as reflections for your personal meditation or journaling, or in a crochet gathering as you consider with others the craft of crochet as contemplation, my hope is that you will find new ways to enrich your spiritual practice and renew your awareness of the connections of creativity to the Spirit. No matter what religious background you come from, I hope you will be able to see crochet in a new light.

Roots and Wings

Soaring while Keeping Our Feet on the Ground

TAKING FLIGHT

My friend Toddy and I were just on the way out the door when something blue caught my eye. There it lay on the walnut table ... a lacy blue purse. I had never seen anything like it! I stopped to gaze, and Toddy explained that she was crocheting it as a gift. She showed me the satiny lining that she hadn't finished sewing yet, and I could see that the completed purse would be wonderful. I was especially awed that someone my own age, at the end of adolescence and barely on the threshold of adulthood, could hold this kind of power and create this kind of beauty.

I thought I knew what crochet was. I had watched my mother crochet simple edgings around towels with cotton thread. I knew my grandmother had hooked a baby sweater for me, and though I couldn't remember observing her in the act of crocheting, she always kept the latest copies of catalogs from yarn companies in her magazine rack. I thumbed through them whenever we visited.

When I was about ten years old, someone gave me a "ponytail hat" kit to make a simple crocheted band with long strands of yarn knotted onto the top and pulled together to make a ponytail. My mother wanted Grandma to teach me how to make it, but my great-grandmother said it would be easier to make it up herself than for someone to teach me. I remember liking the hat, but the colors—yellow and white—left something to be desired—and I didn't learn how to crochet.

That day at Toddy's house, I learned what a crocheted shell stitch looked like, what it looked like in sky blue wool, how sky blue satin contrasted with the rhythms of the shells, and that it was possible to use just yarn and a hook to make something achingly beautiful and useful.

Shell stitch.

It is a mystery to me why no other crocheted objects had moved me until that day. There were plenty of crocheted antimacassars protecting the fabrics on the backs and arms of upholstered furniture in my relatives' homes. I had seen pillowcases with crocheted edgings exchanged as gifts at showers and weddings. Three generations of women in my family had crocheted before me, yet I had never held the hook myself.

Looking back, I wonder how much of the appeal that day was in the beautiful shade of blue. Or the fact that Toddy was one of my peers. Or that the pattern of shells enchanted me. What I do know is this: that day at Toddy's house, stitch pattern, color, and texture all came together and lit up for me.

I remember wishing that Toddy were making the purse for me, but Toddy gave me something more valuable. She taught me how to crochet. She got some yarn and a hook and showed me how to make a square in single crochet. Light again! Deep inside me, there was a creative explosion. In just one stitch were worlds to explore, a depth and breadth of potentialities. As the Chinese philosopher Kuan-tzu so succinctly put it, "Give a man a fish and he eats a meal, but teach him to fish and he eats for a lifetime." Toddy had given me a gift that would "feed" me for a lifetime.

Joseph Campbell, the great student and teacher of mythology, believed that each of us is on our true path when we are doing what our deeper selves want and need to do, what he called following our bliss: "If you do follow your bliss, you put yourself on a kind of track that has been there all the while, waiting for you, and the life that you ought to be living is the one you are living."

When journalist Bill Moyers asked Campbell, "How would you advise somebody to tap that spring of eternal life, that bliss that is right there?" Campbell responded, "We are having experiences all the time which may, on occasion, render some ... little intuition of where your bliss is. Grab it. No one can tell you what it is going to be. You have to learn to recognize your own depth."

My experience of Toddy's crochet as something *beautiful* was, for me, more than "a little intuition" of where my bliss was. The experience of beauty is personal and may even be one of our first experiences that we equate with the Divine. Things we experience as beautiful light up something in us and for us. They touch something deep inside us. They attract us, stay in our memories, and become part of our metaphorical fabric. I like to think of these experiences of beauty as our "wings." They can lift us up and make our spirits soar.

Crochet has given many of us "wings." With the simplest of tools and threads, we can spiral images of birds, flowers, spider webs, and trees into doily forms or onto clothing. We can hold the textures of wonderful fibers in our hands and on our laps. We make colors our own and manifest many forms. We make loops in the air quite literally or as figuratively as a bird.

The beauty of crochet can be captivating. Perhaps you've had the experience of wanting to keep crocheting past dinner, past the laundry that awaits, past bedtime. Or perhaps you had the experience of standing in a yarn shop wanting more: more yarn, more patterns, and more time to try all the projects that catch your eye. After a while, discomfort can settle in, something akin to greed. Lest we fly too high and melt our wings, or become so etheric as to "loose the bonds of earth" (William Blake), we also need to feel our roots.

PUTTING DOWN ROOTS

Learning new skills—being a "beginner" again—helps keep us grounded. An initiate to the craft may hold the strand in one hand and wind it in and out of several fingers. Or maybe make a loop around the pinky. The other hand holds the hook, but which way? The experience of this tool is as new as a child's first attempts at holding a pencil and writing.

The novice crocheter concentrates, keeping the front of the hook turned in the right direction while aiming the point at the yarn supply. The yarn supply, held by the other hand, variously slips and sticks as fingers attempt to control the flow. Each finger has a job to do, but the division of labor is still unclear. Yarn over and pull through, yarn over and pull through, yarn over and pull through a little more gracefully.

The working strand comes from a center-pull ball of yarn. A tangled clump is ejected from the mysterious center. The clump moves closer. Yarn over and pull through confidently. Then, with a gentle yank, the snarling tangle is subdued.

Do you remember your first attempts? Being a beginner is focused work. It keeps us in our bodies. It grounds us. It sends down stabilizing roots. Each time we set out to learn a new stitch, stitch pattern, or technique, we become beginners again. We are reminded that we stand on common ground. As beginners, we start with an act of will that strengthens our ability each time we put it into practice, eventually turning an act of will into an act of beauty. This is the journey of our spiritual lives as well as the journey of our crochet skills: If we concede to always being beginners, we will always be learning something new that can have beautiful results, one stitch at a time.

CROCHET TAKES FLIGHT

Wouldn't you love to have been present the first time someone made a crocheted chain and then turned it back on itself to create that first looped row? Or when someone said, "Oh look, you can make the stitches taller!" From the first finger-hooked chain to the complexity of fine Irish crocheted lace, imaginative, creative minds have sent fingers on grand expeditions into unexplored territory with only one small tool and a very thin rope.

But where did the story begin? Some, believing that a textile art based on such a simple concept as crochet could only be ancient, cling to the possibility that crochet has a long, rich history alongside weaving and knitting. Others have passed on an unsubstantiated story that crochet was known as early as the 1500s by the name of "nun's lace."

In her well-documented volume on the history of crochet, *Crochet: A History and Technique*, Lis Paludan comes to this conclusion: "Because the technique of crochet is uncomplicated and needs just one simple tool, I imagined that its origins went far back in history, and that all I had to do was to track down the relevant sources and material. How wrong I was!... That it proved impossible to find firm evidence of crochet in Europe before 1800 was one surprising result of my research."

Paludan did find and explore two sources from which crochet as we know it today could have arisen. One is *shepherd's knitting*, which consists only of the stitch we know as the slip stitch, worked with a special handmade hook that widens quickly and has the effect of loosening each stitch so it doesn't become too tight to enter when the next row is worked. Shepherd's knitting creates a closed fabric that works well for hats, mittens, and gloves in the cold climes of northern and southeastern Europe, where its use has been documented.

The other possible source of crochet is *tambour work*, a type of chain embroidery that is worked by punching a tool with a tiny crooked end through fabric held in a hoop, pulling up a loop, and then moving forward the length of a chain stitch and punching down again without removing the hook from the loop. This was an ancient form of oriental embroidery in Turkey, Persia, and India that reached Europe in the 1700s. Many believe that it was a short leap of imagination to take away the fabric and make chains in the air.

Still, no one knows. The tambour hook was awkward for crochet and not intended to be used at an angle. The evolution of the hook is a large part of the unknown in the evolution of the crochet craft.

One thing stands out: If it is true that the origins of crochet in Europe cannot be found earlier than 1800, and the path to the beauty of Irish crocheted lace took only another half century, then crochet may be the fastest rising star of all the textile arts!

Early crocheters might have been simply shaping a warm hat or mittens for family members, but by the end of the Victorian era, all manner of Victorian excess was being expressed in crochet. Laces, both thick and thin, became highly developed and were created with a number of different techniques. Baubles and trims ranging from ruffles to dangling crocheted balls edged everything from garments to curtains and then overflowed onto wastebaskets and hampers. Whole ropes of crocheted foliage kept drapes in their place. Tapestry-like designs flowed over filet crochet, and laces went on everything from underwear to babies' bibs.

The pinnacle of crochet, in the minds of many, is Irish crocheted lace. Enabled by the Industrial Revolution and the ability to manufacture fine cotton thread, drawn out by the desire for beauty among those who couldn't afford European laces, and then hastened in its development by dire need for income during the potato famine, Irish crocheted lace reached its peak by the mid-1800s. During the hard times of the famine, cottage industries were set up all over Ireland to teach crochet, so every member of the family could contribute to the work. Because of this extra income, lives were saved just through the use of a crochet hook. The enterprise of crochet gave many of Ireland's poor the ability to survive or to emigrate with the profits of their handwork.

The new lace technique flourished. When Queen Victoria herself was presented with a gift of Irish crocheted laces, she took to wearing them, thereby bestowing the blessing of stylishness on them. To this day, Irish crocheted lace still stands as a summit of productivity and creativity.

Regardless of what we do not know about the history of crochet, we do know this: Crochet represents the work of many hands seeking both warmth and beauty. The tactile connection, the visual interest, the creative satisfaction, and the mysterious beauty we make with our hands not only touch our deepest selves but also link us to the process of creation itself, bringing us closer to our Source.

THE SPIRITUAL LINK

When I told my husband that I was contemplating writing a book about crochet and spirituality, he gave me a response that amounted to a raised eyebrow. Crochet and *spirituality?*

Linking spirituality to craft is not new. As far back as we can trace, individuals and whole societies have poured energy into making useful items beautiful, working with archetypes, weaving in spirit, and making things special for the purpose of ritual. The people of Sumatra, for instance, used to weave images of stylized ships with high prows, stacked cabins, and rows of human and animal figures into wall hangings that were treasured and hung for all rite-of-passage ceremonies. In Peru, beautiful clothing was woven specifically for the burial of the dead. Jewish yarmulkes and Muslim kufis are both types of headwear that symbolize the faith of the wearer and are often crocheted in unique and handsome patterns. Everything from African masks to the great cathedrals, temples, and mosques speaks of the work of hands married to the flight of spirit.

Among Lis Paludan's finds on her journey into crochet's past, and pictured in her book, are two ecclesiastical garments with fine filet crocheted edgings and insertions. Densely stitched double crochet pictures on a foundation of lacy filet mesh express symbols of Christianity and the church. There is also a photograph of an altar cloth with floral crocheted edging worked in fine thread. All three pieces reside at St. Peter's Basilica in Rome and reflect the reach toward Spirit that is present in both the symbols and the beauty of the work.

Several years ago, I came across Matthew Fox's book *Creativity: Where the Divine and the Human Meet*. On reading it, I felt deeply validated in my desire since childhood to make things, to add my own spice to my creations, to garnish as only I could. I felt affirmed about what I have always felt within: in my love and pursuit of crochet, through the work of my hands, I am aligning myself with a source of the Spirit. I am tapping into a nurturing activity that helps me to hear the quiet voice guiding me and leads me to joy through creativity. I am centered.

Fox expresses it this way:

> What happens in meditation is what happens in our acts of creativity: We become united with the Divine Spirit, which is the Spirit of Creation and Creativity.... We con-temple there, that is, we share a sacred temple with the Divine. We call it "contemplation" or unity or forgetfulness of separation and duality. And then creativity surely flows.

Crochet is hands-on meditation. It is intimate, and with it we can create beauty or we can compassionately warm another person. Meditation and intimacy with God, compassion for others—aren't these the concepts that are taught around the globe as responses to the Divine? Through crochet, we can also discover more of who we are and align ourselves with the Mystery of Creation. We can feel our roots and enjoy our flight. Between the threads of our daily rhythms and realities, our spirits can soar.

ROOTS AND WINGS QUERIES

When you were a child, what activities or objects "lit up" a response in you or drew you to them?

What first drew you to crochet? Was it a beautiful object? Or were you attracted to the craft by watching someone ply a hook? What caught your attention?

Think of a crochet experience that has been particularly meaningful. What were the elements that seemed to come together?

What about crochet feels "grounding" for you? When you're crocheting, what makes you feel as if you've "taken flight"?

What is something you perceive as so beautiful that you equate it with the Divine?

Roots and Wings Paperweight

One of the unique traditions of Quaker weddings is the presence of a large certificate, usually penned in calligraphy and illuminated or decorated in some way. Not only do the bride and groom sign the certificate as an integral part of the ceremony, but everyone present either signs the certificate afterward, or has their name signed for them. Everyone present is a witness, a member of the couple's support community.

When my friends Ann and Daniel were planning their wedding—to take place outdoors in a camp setting—one consideration was how to keep the certificate flat (since it would be rolled up in transport to the site, and of course, there might be wind). I visualized some pretty paperweights with lacy tops, special for the occasion, and then made them for Ann and Daniel.

Basically, I ended up making little doilies that topped filled satin pillows. The delicacy of crocheted lace bound to weight. Wings and roots. I started with a central flower motif that I found in a resource book and added flowery clusters around the outer edge that I call "clover picots." I wanted the design to represent things that grow, as I hoped the young people's relationship would grow. (Though I didn't know it then, and wasn't even thinking about the possibility, my own daughter would be the next to use these Roots and Wings Paperweights!)

If you have a little experience with thread crochet and crocheted lace, the lace top as I worked it for Ann and Daniel's wedding is a good project for you. If you are a crochet beginner, I've suggested a simpler alternative below for the top (see Further Ideas at the end of the chapter). You can make one "pillow" to use as a paperweight, or two to hold open the pages of a book, or four to hold down a larger document. Ideas for a variety of uses and styles are also given below.

INTENTION

To make a paperweight with a lacy crocheted top as a reminder that you need both to stay grounded and to grow.

MATERIALS

- 1 ball of size 10 white crochet thread
- size A or B crochet hook (I used a Profi hook.)
- small yarn needle (with an eye large enough to pass the crochet thread through)
- 2 four-inch squares of white fabric
- matching white cotton thread
- sewing needle
- filler (such as plastic pellets)
- scissors

DIRECTIONS

Lace Top

Leaving a 6-inch tail, make a base ring of 6 chains. Join to the first chain with a slip stitch.

Lace top.

Round 1: Chain 5 (this counts as 1 double crochet and 2 chains), [1 double crochet into the ring, chain 2] 7 times, slip stitch to the third chain of the 5-chain (8 spaces).

Round 2: Chain 3 (this counts as 1 double crochet), 4 double crochets into the next chain space, [1 double crochet into the next double crochet, 4 double crochets in next chain space] 7 times, slip stitch to the top of the 3-chain.

Round 3: Chain 3 (this counts as 1 double crochet), [1 single crochet into each of the next 2 double crochet, 1 double crochet into the next stitch, chain 5, skip 1 stitch, 1 double crochet into the next stitch] 7 times. Repeat everything inside the brackets again skipping the last double crochet and slip stitch to the top of the 3-chain.

Ready to pull through all four loops.

Close-up of picot clover.

Round 4: *Note: This round calls for working double crochets together. Here's how to do that: Wrap the yarn around the hook, insert the hook into the next stitch, yarn over, draw up a loop, wrap the yarn again and draw through 2 of the loops on the hook. There will be 2 loops left on the hook. You will repeat these steps in the next 2 stitches, yarn over and pull through all 4 loops.* Chain 3, double crochet 3 together over the next 3 stitches (this counts as double crochet 4 together), [chain 5, 1 single crochet into the next 5-chain arch, chain 5, double crochet 4 together over the next 4 stitches] 7 times. Repeat everything in the brackets again, skipping double crochet 4 together over the next 4 stitches. Slip stitch to the top of the first cluster.

Round 5: *Note: I find it easiest to slip stitch the picots to the last two loops of the double crochet.* Chain 8, [work 3 double crochets together, placing 1 in the next 5-chain arch, 1 in the single crochet, 1 in the next 5-chain arch; chain 5, make 1 double crochet in the top of the next cluster, make 1 picot clover (chain 4, slip stitch, chain 4, slip stitch, chain 4, slip stitch), chain 5] 7 times. Repeat everything inside the brackets again skipping the last chain 5, slip stitch to the third chain of the beginning 8-chain.

Finishing: Thread in the ends of the top. Wash and block your crochet work if you like.

Paperweight Bottom

Make a paper pattern for the bottom. Start with a circle that exactly matches the circumference of the lace top. Add a quarter-inch seam allowance all the way around. You can use a compass if you have one, or simply use a cup or jar lid or refrigerator container lid that is the right size. Cut out your paper pattern.

Pin your pattern to two pieces of fabric (or one that is folded) and cut out around the pattern.

Lay the two fabric circles together with the right sides inside. Leaving a quarter-inch seam allowance, sew around the two pieces using a back stitch.

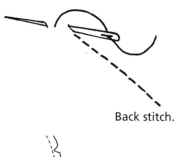

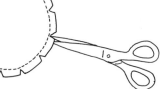

Back stitch.

Leave an unstitched length that will accommodate turning right side out and stuffing. Clip the seam allowance carefully, using only the tips of the scissors.

Turn right side out.

Stuff with plastic pellets. Turn the remaining seam allowance in and sew it closed with small ladder stitches.

Clipping the seam allowance.

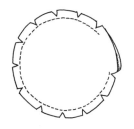

Ladder stitch.　　　Ready to turn right side out.

Assembly

Tack the lace top to the fabric weight. (I like to make small stitches in the two side leaves of the clover picots, leaving the middle picots free.) After sewing all the way around, end with a small knot or several tiny stitches. Then insert the needle close to your knot and exit out the bottom of the fabric weight. Cut the thread close to the weight.

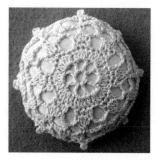

FURTHER IDEAS

- If you are a crochet beginner and need a simpler project, try making a basic granny square for the top of a square paperweight. If you know how to make a granny square but haven't worked with crochet thread, try using a basic granny square pattern but work it in thread and extend it to the dimensions you want. You could sew a ribbon rose on as a finishing touch.

- The lace tops can be used by themselves as coasters. They would make nice gifts at a wedding shower, along with a note about your hopes for "roots and wings" in the couple's marriage.

- White or parchment-colored paperweights with the tops worked in white thread make special gifts for rites of passage, such as weddings, baptisms, and coming-of-age ceremonies.

- Two paperweights, with the bottoms sewn from calico or gingham fabric and the tops worked in a coordinating color, make pretty gifts to hold open cookbooks.

- One weight made with the top and each fabric piece in a different bright, solid color might be just the right gift for a new college student to keep on his or her desk.

2

Plenty

Finding a Sense of Fullness and Gratitude

STORIES OF PLENTY

What is "plenty"? The word represents a quantity, but by what measure? Each of us has a different image of what plenty means. Plenty, like beauty, is a personal experience. For some, plenty might mean having the major needs of life met, such as a sturdy home, food on the table, a healthy neighborhood, and adequate transportation. For others, plenty may be synonymous with *abundance*, having lots of the things we love—which for those of us who crochet might amount to having a generous supply of yarn, hooks, and patterns.

Enough or more than enough? Sufficient or abundant? These are the measures that we apply to our material lives. But when we consider the idea of "plenty" in terms of our spiritual well-being, the word takes on a broader dimension.

When I was teaching First Day School (a Sunday school program in my Quaker meeting), I decided to prepare a lesson on the subject of plenty. I had been thumbing through a book of Native American stories, and a story about plenty caught my attention:

A man named Dayohagwenda cultivated, harvested, and stored his corn carefully, always giving thanks to the Corn Spirit for his bounty. Yet the rest of the villagers had grown careless, trampling the corn stalks, wasting the gleanings, and storing their harvest in poorly made baskets. They forgot to be grateful, to thank the Corn Spirit. Late one autumn, as it became clear that not only the corn, but other food sources as well, were becoming scarce and that the foolishness of the people might lead to starvation, Dayohagwenda went walking in the forest and came upon the Corn Spirit in tattered human form. The young man expressed his respect to the Corn Spirit and begged him not to abandon the people of his village, adding that he would remind them of their responsibilities to the Corn Spirit. Much to his surprise, when Dayohagwenda returned to the village to dig up his own winter corn, he found he was able to feed everyone for the winter from his small supply—and have enough left over for seed corn in the spring! The villagers learned their lesson and never again strayed from their bond to the Corn Spirit.

I began to think about stories of plenty from other traditions. In Greek mythology, there is the story of Zeus and the Horn of Plenty. As an infant, Zeus was protected and fed by a very unusual goat named Amalthea. One day while playing, Zeus accidentally broke off one of Amalthea's horns. As recompense, Zeus promised that the horn would always be filled with whatever good things its owner desired. This became the original cornucopia, or "horn of plenty."

In the Hebrew Bible, there is a story of a widow in debt who was struggling to meet the demands of her husband's creditors. When she told the prophet Elisha that she had nothing left in her house but a little oil, he instructed her to borrow empty jars from her neighbors— and not just a few! She collected jars as she was told, and when she started pouring her oil into them from what she thought was a meager supply, the oil continued flowing until all the jars were filled. She was then able to go out and sell the oil to pay her debts.

In the New Testament Gospels, there is the story of the loaves and fishes, in which Jesus fed five thousand people with just five loaves of bread and two fish. Even though he had spent the day being pursued by people and healing those who were sick, Jesus refused to send the multitude away at mealtime. He blessed and broke the fish and loaves of bread that were available, then asked his disciples to distribute the pieces. According to the book of Matthew, everyone was filled by the food, and the remaining fragments were gathered up in twelve baskets.

Another story of plenty is the one for which Hanukkah is celebrated. After the victory of the Maccabees over King Antiochus IV, a special ritually prepared lamp oil was needed to rekindle the eternal flame on the altar. A single, unopened bottle was all that could be found, and it was only enough to last for one day. But, somehow, the oil continued to burn. Hanukkah, the Jewish festival of lights, is a remembrance of how one day's worth of oil burned for the eight days it took to consecrate fresh oil. During Hanukkah, a candle is lit in the menorah each night to symbolize this miracle of light.

Though these stories come from a variety of traditions, together they give us a broader understanding of the concept of "plenty" than any one story alone. They speak of nurture, of our connection to the earth, and of our relationship with a divine source of goodness.

The Native American story suggests that our sense of plenty comes from our ability to see what we already have, rather than seeing so much of what we want. This story has wonderful elements in it that remind us of the renewability of resources and of faith, the importance of careful craftsmanship, and the place of gratitude in our lives.

The plenty that Zeus made flow from the severed horn reminds us that unexpected good may follow misfortune, and mistakes can be opportunities. One of the first mistakes that beginning crocheters make is to skip stitches, usually at the ends of rows, and when this happens, the work begins to narrow. Yet once we discover that more stitches are needed to keep the sides parallel, we also discover one way to deliberately narrow our fabric—to make triangles, round the crown of a hat, or fit the waist of a sweater. New opportunities are a form of plenty.

The story of the woman who faithfully poured her remaining oil into many jars and sold it to pay her debtors reveals another lesson about plenty: that much can be made from very little. With only tiny amounts of thread, we crocheters can create whole kingdoms of charming motifs. We can turn small amounts of yarn into warming blankets and sweaters. One creative idea can produce a pattern that many can enjoy. As with the woman in the story, faith in divine good and the confidence to act are primary prerequisites.

The story of the loaves and fishes speaks of communion or community. The disciples wanted to dismiss the people, but Jesus understood that breaking bread together was a powerful expression of community. Crocheters share a special form of creative community when we pass on our knowledge of our craft to each other, teach the basics to beginners, and share our colors with the wider world. Plenty abounds when the community is rich in spirit.

Like the other stories, the Hanukkah story tells of unexpected bounty. The gift of light is associated with the Divine in many spiritual traditions, but in this case, light also brought the additional gift of time: enough time to prepare fresh oil and bless it. This story reminds me of the many times I find myself rushing to finish my work. When I slow down and feel time slowing within me, I usually complete everything necessary with time to spare. I am also reminded of the panic that sometimes grips me, the fear that I will come to the end of my strand prematurely and not have enough yarn to finish my project. Occasionally, I do run out of thread or yarn, but more often I am surprised and delighted when I complete my project with length to spare. For me, the Hanukkah story is about a certain trust that what I have will be enough.

AN ORIGINAL PLENTY STORY

Stories often reveal a deeper understanding than we are consciously aware of. As I thought about this idea of plenty, I wrote a story of my own, to see if I could deepen my knowledge of what plenty is and where and how we can find it.

The Magic Horn

Footfalls beat a slow pulse on the misty meadow path. A thin woman in a mended gray cloak will soon be one with a deeper dusk. Ahead in the grass, something to the side of the path catches her eye. A meadow creature? She slows to cautiousness. Its brown bulk appears to be only vegetable matter. She stoops. Like a bird's nest, it is wound and woven of thin, dried vines, small twigs, and brown bits of dry meadow grasses. Colorful heads of small meadow flowers are nestled in the daub that holds all together. But this is not a bird's nest, although it would make a comfortable home for a bird or small beast. The end is elongated; wind and weather, wetting and drying, have curled it, giving the vessel the form of a horn.

The woman stands, cradling the horn in her hands and looking at it with wonder. Balancing its weight in one hand, she explores its depth with the other. Her hand feels no inner wall, only a bit of warmth, a puff of air. She closes her eyes and immediately sees herself standing in a sunlit valley with gardens, orchards, fields, and pastures. Behind relaxed lids, her eyes see cultivated rows, heavy with the produce of the season. Dots and small patches of red, yellow, and orange peek from the leaves of their mother plants. The woman knows these for the jewels they are.

Then the woman's hand wraps around something in the horn that is dense and round. She now finds herself in an orchard. The aroma of ripened fruit, like wine and lightly aged cider, is in her nostrils, and the heady smell of mature fruit draws the bees. The nut trees are also plentiful, and small, hard, woody pieces drop into her hand. The squirrels have taken their winter share, and one little nut cask after another, in excess of the squirrel's need, joins its brothers on the ground waiting for the harvester. The woman is no stranger to the trees and their gifts.

Inside the horn, her hand moves again, and this time she brushes lightly over the tops of many slender plants. "The grains," she thinks, as patchwork plantings of rye, buckwheat, millet, and oats come into view and dance in the breeze before her. Varying shades of brown, tan, and gold catch both sun and wind in ever-changing patterns of light and shade. The woman can taste a good dense bread on her tongue.

There is something warm and soft within the horn now, and the warmth spreads up her arm, across her shoulders, covering her like a new, thick cloak. A grassy, hillside enclosure stretches before her, and sheep dot the hillside. Each member of the flock bears a new woolly load that will be its coat against the winter cold. The woman's old cloak is made from a fleece such as will be cut from these sheep in the warmth of the following spring. The woman knows the creamy color of clean fleece, the loft of teased and carded wool, the firmness of a twisted thread. She has the skill to bring these things about. She hears the call of the sheep in response to the call of the shepherd. It is time to go home to the fold.

Sensing that the Horn of Plenty has worked its final magic, the woman withdraws her hand. Her eyes open slowly on a dawn that is just gathering itself to burst into day. One foot moves as if to step toward the coming sun, but her foot is barred from forward motion. Looking down, to her amazement, she sees an array of the season's best lying about her: the fruits of vine and tree, nuts in abundance, a great sheaf of wheat, and a perfect fleece.

The horn is crumbling, its pieces falling to the ground from the hand that held it. But what is this in her other hand? Unknowingly, her hand has remained clenched around one small remainder from the kingdom within the horn: a seed that is slowly cracking open to reveal the first twin leaves of its potential within. Sensing warmth and a slight tingling in her palm, the woman closes her eyes one last time.

She finds herself in the presence of family and friends and a board spread broadly with bread, soups, and pies. The colors, textures, and aromas of a great feast abound in this humble place; laughter and chatter fill the air. In one corner, a plump basket sits filled with yarn; a bouquet of carved hooks rises from a firmly wound ball. Another basket, covered with colorful cloth, hides completed gifts: warm things for ears, toes, and fingertips, something for everyone.

A movement in the woman's hand brings her sharply back to the meadow. The seed's vine is growing! She places the tiny plant on the ground where its roots can find food. Then she folds the night's harvest into her cloak and, heaving it across her back, turns homeward. With one backward glance, she can see that the mysterious vine already bears the vague form of a cornucopia.

FOOD, FLOWERS, AND FIBER

A quote attributed to the Qur'an says, in effect, we need both bread for our bodies and roses for our souls. This sentiment became part of the rallying cry of the women's labor movement in the early 1900s. James Oppenheim penned the refrain of "bread and roses" into his poem of the same name, which was first published in the *American Magazine* in December of 1911. Mimi Farina later set the poem to music. The title "Bread and Roses" also came to belong to a nationally recognized, award-winning organization that uses the power of performing arts to uplift the human spirit.

Bread is a necessity for our bodies, and roses symbolize the food required for our souls. To this pairing, I would add fiber—which speaks of our need to create warmth and beauty—to form a natural triad that nurtures body and soul. All three invite our senses. All three connect us to life, to growing, to living things. The garden produces not only vitamin- and mineral-laden vegetables but also dye plants, flowers, and roots that are full of pigments. The land provides food for the animals, and animals in turn provide manure that becomes food for the soil, the vitamins and minerals for the garden. Cotton, linen, hemp, ramie, and other fiber plants spring from fertile ground, and the very coats of the animals become our coats.

After I wrote my story "The Magic Horn," I thought more about the yarns I use. The best quality yarns are usually made of natural fibers. I understand that many crocheters are concerned about the expense of natural fiber yarns, their washability, and possible allergic reactions to them. I have used synthetic yarns myself, often out of the same concerns. When I was first designing my Community Crochet patterns for projects that could be donated to charitable organizations, most recipients called for the use of synthetic yarns because they were easier to wash (although, since then, many superwash wool yarns and washable blends have become available). Even now, I frequently make the prototypes for my designs in an inexpensive, synthetic yarn first, in case my ideas don't work out well. Then I feel freer to make the finished project in a more luxurious fiber.

Today, the range of natural fibers available is very broad, and there are good reasons to turn our eyes and our fingertips in the direction of quality natural fibers. One reason in particular is that polyester (acrylic) fibers are manufactured from two chemical products that are derived from oil. However, new synthetics are being invented, and some are being made from renewable products. Rayon fiber is one of those produced from plant material, and new yarns manufactured from the soy plant are also finding a niche. Yet it is difficult for me to see beauty in the factory process necessary to manufacture these products, especially where strong chemicals are involved. It is easier to think of factories taking up the time-consuming jobs of carding and spinning fibers that have grown in sunshine and been fed by the nutrients of the earth. Everything we could want is present in the elasticity of wool, or the firmness of alpaca, the warmth of angora, the coolness of linen, the comfort of cotton.

Perhaps the most important reason to crochet with quality natural fibers is that their sensuality feeds our souls. We crocheters can take pride in the fact that our craft has not yet been and may never be mechanized. It is still an intimate fiber skill, bringing the color of yarns and threads, the pleasure of finishes and twists, and the feel of finished fabric directly into our hands. These things are soul satisfying.

If you have never used yarns you thought were truly beautiful in your crochet—yarns that you wanted to spend time looking at, touching, savoring—I encourage you to try it. Treat yourself to a couple of skeins that you might usually consider "too expensive" and then work them up slowly, taking in the pleasure of your fabric as it unfolds in front of you. Fill your senses with the true plenty of natural beauty.

CRAFT OF PLENTY

When I consider the craft of crochet, I am reminded of the sense of fullness that the word *plenty* evokes. A crocheter always has abundant possibilities. We have stitches of at least three different heights, and a variety of fabrics can evolve from each one. We can easily add texture to our projects by working shells, bobbles, popcorns, chains, and cables. Items as sturdy and stiff as bowls or soft and fine as babies' blankets come away from our busy hooks. Lacework and doilies emerge with fine thread and small hooks. Wind- and weather-tight accessories are born of thick wool and thick hooks. Variations in the three steps of insert hook, yarn over, and pull through are all we need. With its ease of design, crochet invites us to a feast of creativity.

Once, in the "early morning" of my crochet life, bobbles and a skein of bulky, heather-pink yarn taught me a lesson about plenty. I had found my skein, a trusted quality in fiber and twist, in a department store in upstate New York while I was home for a visit. Pink has always been one of my favorite colors, and I have found that using heathers, created from different colors or different shades of the same color carded together before they are spun, is one of the simplest ways to make projects interesting. I didn't have a particular project in mind for my skein, but I was taken with this heather-pink yarn and treated myself to it.

Back in Tennessee, I decided I would make a young child's bonnet. It would consist of a rectangle from ear-to-ear and a square shape down the back of the head. I planned to use a basic stitch and keep it simple. I wasn't a fan of high texture.

A feminine necktie, two small purses, and a baby blanket worked from corner to corner.

Things didn't go well at first. The yarn had nice loft, but when I crocheted with it, the results looked knotted and tight. The beautiful yarn didn't have a chance to fluff up and show off its softness! One problem was my hook, and a friend offered to whittle some larger hooks from dowels. While I waited for my new hooks, I started to play with popcorns and bobbles. The voluptuousness of my yarn certainly seemed to call for something less restrained than basic stitches. I liked the bobbles best, and to my surprise, they seemed to release the beauty of the fibers.

When my oversized hooks were ready, I felt completely at ease proceeding with my child-sized hat. I don't remember exactly what it looked like when it was finished, but I do remember that a neighbor who was an artist asked if she could buy it for her daughter. She had an artist's eye, she liked it, and she paid me for it.

And I also remember this: my yarn told me what it needed. It needed more than I originally planned to give, more room to fill the spaces between the stitching, more texture to show off subtle shading. It begged for plenty. When I listened, its spirit of beauty could shine through.

YOUR "STASH OF PLENTY"

If you're new to crochet, you probably don't have this particular problem but I have known weavers, knitters, and crocheters to accumulate bags of yarn in their closets, boxes in their garages, and handfuls in cupboards. Some have a guest bedroom in their home that ceases to allow much space for a guest. The luckiest among us have a designated studio. I have one of those—in my imagination.

For many of us, our stash represents the colors and textures of a flower garden right under our roof. There are the red and red-orange skeins: a lightweight cotton boucle; a terra-cotta lamb's wool; a fuzzy, fingering weight mohair just waiting to become a shawl. Next to the reds might be the green skeins: a blue-green alpaca; a green and tan wool-blend twist; a pale, spring-mist angora. Oh, the yellows! They are the most difficult to find. Yet here they are in shades of butternut, maple leaf, marigold, and mum.

"Plenty" needs to be organized. Karen Klemp, past president of the Crochet Guild of America, works with crocheters on how to think about the yarn flow that comes into their living spaces. She encourages us to think about our habits of buying yarn and squirreling it away, and she has several concrete tips that she has generously allowed me to share.

Karen remembers noticing that her grandmother's yarns, which were stored in the plastic shopping bags in which they came home from the store, tended to get something related to dry rot. Karen doesn't shy away from using plastic for storage, even for wool, but she moves her newly purchased yarns to food-quality storage bags and squeezes the air out before sealing them—a sort of do-it-yourself method of vacuum preservation.

Another tip Karen offers is that if you've purchased a quantity of yarn for a particular pattern, you should "swatch"* your yarn immediately upon bringing it home. That way, if it becomes clear that your yarn won't work for the pattern you've chosen, you can return the rest of it, and it won't become an accidental part of your stash. If, after making a swatch, the yarn continues to feel appropriate and works to the gauge, store the pattern with the bag of yarn, making a note of the size and brand of hook with which you made your swatch.

Karen also advises against storing yarn "on the periphery." When yarn collections are stored in attics, garages, and basements, they receive the least care and are the least likely to be used eventually.

Here are a few of my own thoughts about caring for your yarn collection:

- Arrange your yarns by brand, fiber content, weight, or color, depending on your needs. You can subdivide

---

*A swatch is a sample of fabric made with the hook and in the stitch pattern you intend to use with the yarn. A swatch enables you to know whether a particular yarn and hook will work to the gauge and also gives you an idea of what characteristics the finished piece will have.

within those categories. For example, you might have one shelf of a bookcase designated for a certain brand of yarn and then place the yarn in pull-out baskets organized by weight or by color.

- If you don't have floor space, you can hang your yarns on a rack. You might want to keep your prettiest yarns visible. You could also hang plain canvas bags on pegs for yarn storage that will look tidy. Hang labels from chains of colored yarn so you know what is in them at a glance. You can also package ongoing projects this way, and they will always be ready to take along when you travel.

- I like to wrap ongoing projects in pretty scarves I find at used clothing stores. I bring two opposite corners in and fold them down several times, and then I tie the other two corners together. This method makes a pretty and simple carryall that can be opened up and laid flat while you are working.

- If you want to store your yarns long term, you might "vacuum pack" them as Karen does before placing them in your baskets, bags, and boxes.

- Accessories such as scissors, stitch markers, and yarn needles should have their own home near your yarn. It is a good idea to make up two or more kits of these tools so that they are together when you need a take-along set. If that set gets accidentally left behind somewhere, you will still have your kit at home.

I have access to several excellent yarn catalogs and a local yarn store just a few miles away. Lately, I only go out to buy yarn or order it when I am ready to make a specific project. That way, someone else tends my stash, and I have more free space in my house. For the time being, that is plenty for me.

GRATITUDE

Here's something to think about: German cosmologists believe our universe could be shaped like a horn of plenty. According to *New Scientist Today*, "a funnel shaped universe best explains the pattern of cosmic background radiation observed when the universe was only about 380,000 years old." Today, as we face one ecological crisis after another, we are finally waking up to the idea that we are depleting our planet of plenty. And, thankfully, many are responding with a long-overdue gratitude to our earth for the way it supports us.

Whether our plenty consists of our world of oceans and air, our store of material goodness, our stash of yarn, or the treasure of our inner lives, how we use our plenty reflects our gratitude.

In the Native American story about the Corn Spirit, both the man and his people were surprised by the abundance of food in the young man's stores, after he asked the Corn Spirit for help. There was enough to feed the entire village. In gratitude, the people agreed never again to take the Corn Spirit for granted.

In "The Magic Horn," the woman didn't ask for anything, yet much was given. Gratitude shone in her appreciative use of the food and fiber, and in her sharing of a festive meal and warming gifts with family and friends.

Gratitude, appreciation, and thankfulness all register decidedly on the scale of our spiritual well-being. To be spiritually healthy, to be happy—even joyful—we need to be appreciative and to share our plenty with others. Matthew Fox, author of *Creativity: Where the Divine and Human Meet*, says that, "When gratitude reigns, energy reigns. When thankfulness is real, praise happens. Praise is never lazy. Praise extends itself, sacrifices, gives away. Praise is effusive: it goes out to others."

If we think of creativity as another gift of plenty, sharing our creativity is an expression of our appreciation. Fox tells us, "At the heart of all creativity there lies praise, there lies a hidden 'thank you,' a yearning to return blessing for blessing." How can we find ways to be grateful, to give thanks consciously and regularly as we set our fingers to our crochet work? Perhaps with a moment of silence before picking up yarn and hook. Or with the ringing of a little bell to signal the meditation of the work about to begin. Or with a seed dropped into a bowl, a short blessing to signify gratitude for the tools and materials.

The twin practices of being grateful and expressing gratitude are health giving and soul nurturing. They are the perfect responses to plenty.

PLENTY QUERIES

What does plenty mean to you? Where in your life do you have a sense of plenty?

How does your sense of plenty change under varying circumstances?

Could plenty be something you already have that just requires a different perspective? What would that something be?

How does your sense of plenty make you feel? Satisfied? Secure? Generous? Guilty?

When you crochet, how aware are you of the cycle of growth? Do you work with seasonal colors? Do you use some fibers from natural sources?

What comes to mind when you think of gratitude in your life, in general? In your craft? How do you express that gratitude?

Horn of Plenty "Deskie"

The horn as a symbol of plenty has been recognized since at least the fifth century BCE, and it has found visual expression as a centerpiece during our national holiday of Thanksgiving. But you don't need to wait until November to allow its message to sound. You can make this little yarn cornucopia as a daily reminder of the gifts you have been given. Place a Horn of Plenty "Deskie" on your desk, make several as favors for a small crochet party, or make one as an inexpensive gift for a "yarn" friend.

INTENTION

To make a cornucopia as a reminder to be grateful for the plenty in your life by caring for it and using it generously.

MATERIALS

- 2 skeins (16 yards each) of number 3 perle cotton in color numbers 420 and 869 (You will be working with both colors as if they were one strand.)
- size D crochet hook (I used a Susan Bates hook.)
- yarn needle
- scissors
- 2 four-inch square pieces of good quality wool felt (They can be the same color or complementary colors.)
- 1 four-inch square of cardboard
- 1 yard of embroidery floss, in a contrasting color to the felt
- sewing needle
- small amounts of fine weight yarn (You can use baby fingering weight yarn, sock yarn, or a single strand of needlepoint wool. Using needlepoint wool increases your color options.)
- fabric glue

DIRECTIONS

Notes:

- Because perle cotton comes in small, looped skeins, it will be easier to work with if you roll the skeins into balls before starting this project.

- "Increase 1" means to make 2 single crochets in the stitch below.

- When you make a slip stitch, make it loosely so that it will be easier to enter when you work the next row.

- When your starting tail is on the right, you are looking at the right side of the work.

- You will work your horn of plenty back and forth in rows, making a flat piece, and then sewing it together.

- The completed "Deskie" is about 3½ inches in diameter. The cornucopia is about 2 inches in length.

The finished "Deskie" fits in your hand.

Horn

Leaving a 12-inch tail, chain 5.

Row 1: Single crochet in the second chain from the hook and in each chain across, turn (4 stitches).

Row 2: Chain 1, single crochet in the first stitch of the row below, increase 1 (by making 2 single crochets) in each of the next 2 stitches, single crochet in last stitch, turn (6 stitches).

Row 3: Chain 1, single crochet in next stitch, increase 1 in next stitch, single crochet in each of the next 2 stitches, increase 1 in next stitch, single crochet in next stitch, turn (8 stitches).

Row 4: Chain 1, single crochet in each of the next 2 stitches, slip stitch in each of next 4 stitches, single crochet in last 2 stitches, turn (8 stitches).

Row 5: Chain 1, single crochet in next stitch, increase 1 in next stitch, single crochet in next 4 stitches, increase 1 in next stitch, single crochet in last stitch, turn (10 stitches).

Row 6: Chain 1, single crochet in next stitch, increase 1 in next stitch, single crochet in each of the next 6 stitches, increase 1 in next stitch, single crochet in last stitch, turn (12 stitches).

Row 7: Chain 1, single crochet in next stitch, increase 1 in next stitch, single crochet in each of the next 2 stitches, slip stitch in each of the next 4 stitches, single crochet in each of the next 2 stitches, increase 1 in next stitch, single crochet in last stitch, turn (14 stitches).

Row 8: Chain 1, single crochet in next stitch, increase 1 in next stitch, single crochet in each of the next 10 stitches, increase 1 in next stitch, single crochet in last stitch, turn (16 stitches).

Row 9: Chain 1, single crochet in each of the next 6 stitches, slip stitch in each of the next 4 stitches, single crochet in each of the last 6 stitches, turn (16 stitches).

Row 10: Chain 1, single crochet across. End off leaving a 14-inch tail.

Finishing: Thread the starting tail into a yarn needle. Stitch through each loop of the starting row and pull up to close the end. With the right side out, use an overcast stitch to sew the side edges together, catching only one strand on each side. Thread the end to the inside and trim.

Use an overcast stitch to sew side edges together.

Thread the ending tail into your yarn needle and overcast stitch through both loops of every stitch in the last row. Thread the end inside the horn and trim.

Shape the horn with your fingers. Your thumb may make a good mold inside the horn. Smooth over it with the fingers of the other hand. Spread a line of fabric glue or fabric stiffener just along the seam to help maintain the curve.

Base

Overcast stitch.

While your horn is drying (you might want it to dry overnight), cut two circles of felt about 3½ inches in diameter (or larger, if you wish). You can use a cup or jar lid to trace your circles.

Next, cut a piece of cardboard about ¼-inch smaller all around than your felt circles.

Cut a length of contrasting embroidery floss long enough to lay around your circle, loosely, three times. Divide the strands of the floss in half (embroidery floss has six strands) and thread three strands into a sewing needle. (You can set aside the remaining three strands for another use.) Use an overcast stitch to sew the two felt circles together, with the cardboard sandwiched in between.

Miniature Yarn Balls

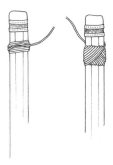

Making a pretty miniature ball of yarn.

Using your fine weight yarn, make three tiny balls to go inside your horn. You can wind them around a pencil as shown in the illustrations. When you have made three yarn balls that fit, glue them to the inside edge of your horn with fabric glue.

Assembly and Decoration

Glue your horn to the felt base. Now make two more decorative balls of yarn around your pencil. After winding one, pull it off the pencil and cut it free, leaving enough of a tail to glue to the base. Wind the second ball. Put a dab of glue on each ball to keep it from unwinding. (It helps to use the end of a toothpick to apply the glue.) Glue each ball to the base and then glue its tail to the base, forming an interesting curve.

If you like, you can file down a toothpick to suggest a tiny crochet hook.

FURTHER IDEAS

- Make a Horn of Plenty "Deskie" as a gift of thanks to give to someone for whom you are grateful.

• Make a larger horn of plenty with heavier thread or yarn and a larger hook. You can sew two wooden beads to the underside for balance instead of attaching it to a base. Fill this vessel with small pieces of paper on which you write the things you are grateful for. Writing down the material goods you treasure, the opportunities you have been offered, and the plenty you feel is a good exercise to practice by yourself or with a crochet group, where each person contributes one thing she is thankful for.

• Purchase a full-sized basket cornucopia and fill it with balls of yarn and small crochet projects, or include just a hook and a bit of crocheted fabric. Use this arrangement as a centerpiece. You don't have to wait for Thanksgiving; the story of the horn of plenty is a timeless one.

3

The Power of Limits

Having More within a Structure of Less

MORNING GLORIES

My mind is on morning glories.

Morning glory vines often find their way into spent summer gardens and an assortment of other sunny yet weedy spots. Once they have taken root, they climb on every crisp brown stalk they can find. They "grow like weeds" and, because they arrive and proliferate so freely, are often seen and treated as weeds—despite the beauty of their blooms and their practical appeal to hummingbirds, bees, and butterflies. So I was surprised one childhood summer when my mother deliberately put a trellis next to our house and planted a row of morning glory seeds beneath it.

Freed from their randomness of place and position, given their own real estate, and having their climbing needs met; being limited to a line and a lattice, they became flowers. Each little sunshine pistil inside of its own blue-sky blossom said "good morning" from its place of order. The vines were no longer relegated to bent and aging tomato plants as supports. Now blooms met me face to face from high on their tendril-friendly trellis.

I could have asked my mother, "Why do you want to plant them here, against the side of the house, when they seem to grow all over the place? The roses and peonies and hydrangea all know their

35

places. Why give the lowly morning glories this place of honor?" But I didn't ask those questions; I just watched. A lattice, a limit, a foundation is a place from where excess can easily be trimmed, all can be seen, and the clockwork lives of morning glories can instill wonder. It is only now that this image of morning glories limited to a trellis gives tangible form to my understanding of the power of limits. It is only now that I understand that removing the chaos of randomness and instituting order is a form of empowerment.

Order is one of the tools we use to limit the chaos in our lives. Most of us prefer restful, visual tidiness at times. I suspect that part of the joy of spending the night in a good hotel room is that the room isn't full of accumulated stuff!

Part of the enjoyment of any empty space is in the potential for filling and arranging it. Some of the most interesting people I know live in small spaces filled with what looks like clutter at first glance; but these people can put their fingers on anything they need. I think of a crochet designer who makes crochet magic in a New York City apartment, where she makes use of every wall, from floor to ceiling. I know a writer who inhabits an office filled with thick tomes on tall, dark shelves and in twisted piles, giving an observer to believe that some ancient sage studies there. Then I think of my friend whose house is in constant fluctuation because she loves to try different painting techniques on her walls, floors, and furniture. So I am not suggesting we need picture-perfect order! I am suggesting *just enough* order so we can live out our creative lives fully and with the least frustration.

But order isn't only about decluttering our environment and applying feng shui principles, although both can help us achieve a sense of peace. Order is empowering. Our inner lives need order as much as our outer lives. We need to feel good about ourselves, and our relationship to creation and Creator. We need to attend lovingly to our foundation of calm and confidence. We need time alone, a place of our own—even if that place is no more than a favorite chair.

Setting priorities is one way to instill order and to limit excess. What one chore, when completed, would best free me and other family members to pursue our goals? Who needs or would most like to hear from me? What steps do I need to take to finish one crochet project: thread in ends, sew seams, or purchase buttons? Which project would best calm me and remind me to hand over some responsibility to divine guidance? Setting priorities means doing what most needs doing and relaxing about the rest.

Setting material priorities can help limit material excess. My husband and I both work with our hands, so we share an understanding that tools and materials for creative work are a priority. A whole range of financial arguments are kept at bay with that one unspoken agreement. As a crocheter and a crochet designer, I need hooks, yarns, and resource books; as an author, I need plenty of notebooks, paper, and a good computer. For his hobby, my husband needs cameras, camera accessories, photo paper, and a lot of printer ink. To allow for our creative lives, we often choose to purchase our clothes at used clothing stores and forgo live entertainment. We set limits to empower our creative practices.

One of the prerequisites for setting priorities is focus, and it may be the most difficult challenge. When we want to focus on a crochet project, for example, many things clamor for our attention: the day's to-do list, the family's needs, the week's commitments to school or work or community. The chattering monkey in our minds must be sent back to his jungle, and the voices of others—even friends and family—must sometimes be put on hold so we can tend to our purpose.

Order, priority, and focus are three important means of tapping into the power of limits, but there are two other tools we can add to the equation: silence and simplicity. Just as we might tend to think of limits as restrictive rather than empowering, so, too, might we think of silence and simplicity as subtractions rather than additions. Yet their very limitations have enormous positive value.

Silence and simplicity are the gems that lie just beneath the surface of our daily lives. We have only to brush away a bit of the day's surface to recognize the sheen of their presence. The more we uncover them, the brighter they shine. They are free for the taking. Though uncovering them may require some work, by gently, consciously, and consistently limiting the unnecessary things that hide them, we can discover their true wealth.

SILENCE

My first lessons in the value of silence came when I started to explore the craft of crochet as a young adult—not as a complete or disciplined silence, but as a form of stillness. In those early days, I crocheted alone and without the added stimulation of radio or television. The quiet setting allowed me to experience my surroundings more intensely.

I remember hearing birdsong and neighborhood noises, an occasional train in the distance, and I was charmed by the almost imperceptible whisper of hook against fiber. I saw sunshine warming everything outside my window, brightening the white sill inside and turning the wood-grained floor gold. I still remember the colors of my yarn rolled into balls in a basket, then taking shape in my lap. That quieting seemed larger than myself; I felt secure in it. The accompanying rhythm of crocheting was like easy rocking, and I often rose from my work as from a good meal or a good night's sleep.

Deeper lessons in silence came as I learned the discipline of worshiping in a traditional Quaker meeting. There, the silence was shared with others. When my young friend Dolly invited me to attend my first meeting, I was introduced to meditative silence as worship. Traditional Quakers enter the meeting in silence and keep a reverent silence between them for the purpose of listening: listening for the Presence in the midst, the Divine, the still, small voice within. The silence is broken only by the occasional person delivering a carefully listened-for spiritual message.

Extended silence is also the spiritual foundation of a number of monastic orders in the Catholic Church; many monks and nuns, though they do not take a vow of silence, practice silence. Thomas Merton, a Trappist monk well known for his ecumenism and his writings, said, "It is in deep solitude and silence that I find the gentleness with which I can truly love my brother and sister."

In many other traditions, silence is honored as well. Among the best-known stories of silent teachings is that of the Buddha's "flower sermon." The Buddha's disciples were settling in to hear a lesson when the Buddha simply reached into a pond and pulled up a lotus. He held it up for all to see but said nothing. His message was in the silence. Another spiritual leader, Mahatma Gandhi, said of silence, "In the attitude of silence, the soul finds the path in a clearer light." And the Quaker William Penn once wrote, "True silence is the rest of the mind; it is to the spirit what sleep is to the body, nourishment and refreshment."

As I have been writing this book, a film has been released that captures the powerful music of silence in a Carthusian monastery in the French Alps. Almost three hours of film time are dedicated to the day-to-day, month-to-month sounds of the cycles of nature and of the life within this strict order. (Talking is permitted only on weekends and when absolutely necessary.) *Into Great Silence* has drawn larger than expected audiences and may be a signal of how much we long for a soothing balm in our noisy world of electronic signals. The film's producer, Philip Groening, says of his experience in filming it, "The silence taught me a new kind of patience: if you haven't got the image you want to film at that moment, if you keep waiting a little longer, something of incredible beauty will show up, an image that you weren't even looking for." This can happen with our crochet work and any other artistic or craft endeavor: silence teaches patience; and patience makes room for beauty.

Over time, my own experience of silence has seeped into me and deepened. It is not only part of my Quaker worship, but I now carry it within: to work, into the out-of-doors and into other religious settings. It informs my crocheting. Though there is more technology around me now than there ever was when I was young, I still choose to crochet in silence when I am in the house alone. That is when I best hear the voice of creativity, see colors from a deeper place, and hold people prayerfully in my mind as I crochet.

While many crocheters like to crochet while doing other things, such as listening to music or books on tape, or watching television with the family, I recommend some regular time of crocheting in silence. If you meet with a group of crocheters, you might consider introducing some silence into your gathering. Try a ten-minute period of silence at the start of each meeting and then allow a few minutes more for sharing your experience of the silence. Let conversation unfold slowly afterward so the change is not abrupt. You might be surprised at the gifts even a short period of silence brings.

You could start your silent time with a reading about silence, such as this one from *A Quaker Book of Wisdom:*

> Silence is as common as the air we breathe. It is a vast pool always available to us where we can refresh and renew ourselves, or simply stop in for a while. Silence is God's gift to our minds, a gift that modern life seems to have lost or crowded out. We need more silence in our lives, more stillness in our homes. We need, in our increasingly complex and frenetic world, to silence ourselves—and to listen.

SIMPLICITY

Some think of simplicity only as a form of material denial. Some equate voluntary simplicity with voluntary poverty. We may envision simple living as breaking away from modern appliances and other technological advances. At its best, simplicity is enriching rather than impoverishing, empowering rather than denying.

Simplicity is about taking charge of our lives, balancing soul needs of all kinds with material needs, finding the proper proportion for each. For every item we bring into our dwelling places, there are connected factors of organizing, storing, and maintaining those items. Likewise, there is the ever-present question of what we could be doing with the same amount of money, energy, and time we spend on our possessions that might better serve our inner lives, our families, and our communities.

Simplicity may involve challenging ourselves to limit the material bulk we live with, but it is also about doing so with purpose. In 1936, Richard Gregg, a student of Gandhi's, published an article called "Voluntary Simplicity," in which he wrote:

> Voluntary simplicity involves both inner and outer condition. It means singleness of purpose, sincerity and honesty within, as well as avoidance of exterior clutter, of many possessions irrelevant to the chief purpose of life. It means ordering and guiding our energy and our desires, a partial restraint in some directions in order to secure greater abundance of life in other directions. It involves a deliberate organization of life for a purpose.

For me, simplicity cannot be separated from the work of my hands. When I gather my supplies and set aside time to crochet, I am taking charge, perhaps unconsciously, of many important connections in my life. My hands are involved in meeting my needs, rather than allowing machines to do that for me, and I am less likely to succumb to consumer frenzy. I develop a sense of independence, a special knowing that, if necessary, I could make needed household goods and warm clothing. I am expressing my individuality. If my psyche demands a red and purple striped hat, I don't have to wait for fashion trends to change before I make that gift for my inner being! Perhaps most important, I am exercising my creativity. I am tapping into that vein of wealth that ties me to a vastly creative universe.

From the simplicity of a few stitches, I am empowered not only in being able to make the things I need and want, but also in a larger process of learning. As I practice, I learn to accept my shortcomings, fix my mistakes, and see my projects to completion. I learn patience and management. And because I have seen how one stitch at a time can make a blanket, I am not a stranger to the idea of taking one step at a time when faced with solving a life problem or just making it through a rough day.

The Quaker community has a particular take on simplicity, just as we do with silence. No rules are passed down from a hierarchy, but rather we take a democratic approach that encourages each person to seek a level and form of simplicity that is guided by that individual's conscience. In *A Quaker Book of Wisdom*, Robert Lawrence Smith addresses this approach beautifully: "For Friends, the word 'simple' describes a way of life that follows naturally from a way of worshiping. All you need to worship is a quiet place or a plain Meetinghouse. All you need for living are a few possessions, simplicity of spirit, and readiness to answer to the divine spark in every person."

PROPORTION

Both silence and simplicity are limits that speak to the broader picture of balance in our lives. In order to keep our lives in balance, we each need the ratio of sound and silence, "stuff" and simplicity that works for us. We need to seek the right proportion of our outer resources—such as time, money, and material goods—to our inner resources—our passions, our wisdom, and our best understanding of how to share our gifts with others. When we carve away excess and keep balanced proportions of both the outer and the inner, we can sculpt lives of beauty that reveal the hidden forms of our inner selves.

In the world of nature, proportion is an amazing study. Have you ever heard of something called the Fibonacci sequence? Even if you don't consider yourself a "math person," it's worth a few moments of your time to grasp this amazing fundamental organizing factor of our world.

Back in 1202, Italian mathematician Leonardo of Pisa, also known by the name Fibonacci, introduced to the West a sequence of numbers that have been called "nature's numbering system." The numbers appear everywhere in the natural world—in leaf arrangements, flower petals, the scales of a pineapple, bee colonies. Simply put, the Fibonacci sequence is a series of numbers where each one is the sum of the previous two:

$$0 + 1 = 1$$
$$1 + 1 = 2$$
$$1 + 2 = 3$$
$$2 + 3 = 5$$
$$3 + 5 = 8$$
$$5 + 8 = 13$$
$$8 + 13 = 21$$
$$13 + 21 = 34$$

The resulting series—1, 2, 3, 5, 8, 13, 21, 34—goes on ad infinitum.

The next time you look at a flower, count the number of petals; most likely the number will be one of the Fibonacci numbers: 1-petal calla lily, 2-petal euphorbia, 3-petal iris, 5-petal columbine, 8-petal delphinium, 13-petal black-eyed Susan, 21-petal Shasta daisy. If you pick an ordinary field daisy, it has 34 petals—a fact to keep in mind if you're playing, "He loves me, he loves me not"!

These numbers not only make some intriguing patterns in nature, but they can produce some balanced patterns in crochet. You can create pleasing stripe patterns using these Fibonacci numbers. Try crocheting a scarf or a pillow using two colors and varying the width of the stripes using the Fibonacci numbers (1, 2, 3, 5, and/or 8 rows each).* Try different combinations of rows using these numbers. You can also experiment with more than two colors or play with contrasting textures.

---

*In back-and-forth single crochet, it is a good idea to count the two rows between the horizontal furrows as one, because changing colors between those two rows will change the texture and inhibit your enjoyment of the stripe proportion.

There's another element of beauty in these numbers that has implications for living things and human-made creations alike, something mathematicians call "the golden proportion." In *The Power of Limits*, Gyorgy Doczi describes the mathematical harmony of the golden proportion as a limiting factor that produces dynamic symmetry in nature. Mathematically, the proportion is a ratio of 1 to 1.618 (which comes from dividing each number in the Fibonacci sequence by the number that comes before it). The results are called the "golden ratio" (*phi* = 1.618), and the ramifications are complex and wonderful!

This ratio is found in the growth patterns of plants, in the spiral of the nautilus, in the double-helix of DNA. If you slice through a cabbage or an apple, or study the florets in the centers of daisies or sunflowers, the patterns reveal an underlying proportion that exists throughout nature. And when we humans use the golden proportion in building, we create some of our most beautiful structures, such as the Parthenon and the Cathedral at Chartres.

For crocheters, the golden proportion is another great design element to experiment with: we can make "golden rectangles"! Once you know how to crochet a simple granny square, you can make varied design patterns using this principle. The basic principle is that the side of each new square must equal the sum of the sides of the previous two squares:

First, make two equal-sized squares:

Then make a third square (whose side is the sum the previous two):

Then a fourth square (whose side is the sum of
the previous two):

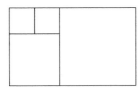

You can keep adding the squares, making each
new square's side a sum of the two previous
squares' sides, and you'll have constructed a
golden rectangle:

Once you try crocheting something designed in this golden proportion, it will come as no surprise to you that the proportion is also
sometimes called the divine proportion. It is pleasing to the eye,
and it can provide plenty of entertainment if you like to play with
design ideas. The golden proportion is a powerful limit, a foundation on which you can play with color and rhythm while creating
something with warmth and visual appeal.

There are many ways to apply the power of limits to our crochet. You might decide to make stripes in only one color but use different stitch patterns. Or you might work a project in many variations of one color using only smooth yarns, so the subtle color changes are the focus. Or you might crochet a pillow or purse with only one wide stripe in the center and embellish it with creative details.

The limits we establish in our craft—and in our lives—open up new vistas. They change our focus, narrow it with purpose, and allow us to find subtle and beautiful variations in the way we live and the way we crochet. This is the power of limits.

POWER OF LIMITS QUERIES

Think of an example in your life when a limit actually created a richer experience for you. How did you first feel about the imposition of a limit? Looking back, what can you see were the benefits of this limit?

Do you pursue a meditative practice that helps you focus your energies? How does your crocheting help you focus?

What have you learned about limits from your crochet activities? What does that tell you about yourself?

How might your purchasing be different if you always considered the question, what do I really need? What might change if you ranked uncluttered space, quiet time, and creative growth as important as clothes and groceries?

Think of an object that you love especially because it has beautiful proportions. What makes it beautiful in your eyes?

Think of something you find especially beautiful because of its usefulness. How are its proportions also beautiful?

Morning Glory Motif

Morning glories, when they open to the sun, unfold as a single unit rather than a cluster of petals. Their blooms display five points, a Fibonacci number, and their pentagonal proportions exemplify the golden proportion. Making Morning Glory Motifs is a way to make a visual expression of this harmonious proportion.

INTENTION

To make a Morning Glory Motif to remind yourself of the value of limits and the need for a foundation of calm and quiet, beauty and simplicity.

MATERIALS

- 1 skein each of yellow, white, and morning glory blue worsted weight yarn
- crochet hooks in sizes G and H (I used Susan Bates hooks.)
- yarn needle for threading in ends and attaching motifs
- scissors

DIRECTIONS

Pistil

With yellow yarn and a size G hook, leave a 6-inch tail and chain 3, half double crochet in the second chain from the hook, slip stitch in the last chain. Leave a 6-inch tail. Cut yarn, pull through. (I like to make several pistils before I start my morning glories. Directions for attaching them come later.)

Bloom

With white yarn and a size G hook, chain 4 and join with a slip stitch to form a ring.

Round 1: Chain 2 (counts as 1 half double crochet), work 1 half double crochet in the ring, chain 1, (make 2 half double crochets in the ring, chain 1) 4 times, join with a slip stitch to the top of chain 2. End off.

Round 2: Change to a size H hook and blue yarn. Pull up a loop in any chain-1 space, chain 3, 1 double crochet in the same space, chain 1, 2 double crochets in the same space (first corner), 1 double crochet in between the 2 half double crochets below, *2 double crochets in the next chain-space, chain 1, 2 double crochets in the same chain-space, 1 double crochet between the 2 half double crochets below. Repeat from asterisk 3 more times (5 corners); join to top of chain 3 and break off.

Round 3: Pull up a loop in any chain-1 corner space, work first corner as for round 2, then skip stitch, 1 double crochet in the last double crochet of the corner below, 1 half double crochet in the 1 double crochet below, 1 double crochet in the first stitch of the next corner below, *work next corner, 1 double crochet in last stitch of corner below, 1 half double crochet in double crochet below, 1 double crochet in first stitch of corner below. Repeat from asterisk 3 more times; join and break off.

Double crochet, half double crochet, and double crochet between corners.

Finishing: Place the pistil in the center of the white section. On the back, pull each tail through a loop of a stitch on either side of the ring, tie the 2 strands in a knot and thread in the ends. Thread in the remaining ends and trim.

You can use the ending threads to attach motifs to each other. Just thread each one out to the chain that is a point of the flower, make two stitches to secure the two motifs and thread the end in snugly.

Pentagonal shapes meander,
rather than form a straight line.

FURTHER IDEAS

• Make Morning Glory Motifs in different sizes by changing yarn and hook sizes. Use them individually or in groups. Try making them in the full range of morning glory colors, or just in that beautiful blue they seem to come in most often.

• Make a scarf that is one Morning Glory Motif wide by joining the motifs at two adjacent points. In this case, the motifs will meander randomly rather than form a straight line. You might try curving three in one direction and then three back in the other direction to create a lightly undulating effect.

• Try attaching any number of Morning Glory Motifs to a simple mesh shawl. Make the motifs in sport weight yarn for a size that is closer to the real thing.

• Use a variety of thread weight strands to create morning glory pins and add-ons for garments, hats, and bags.

Meditation Meets Prayer

Two Practices in One

MANY WAYS UP THE MOUNTAIN

The name Baba Ram Dass might bring to mind images of a holy man wrapped in lengths of white cotton, or a statue of a god with more than the human limitation of two arms and two hands. Yet Baba Ram Dass is the name conferred on Dr. Richard Alpert, an American, well educated in the social sciences and one-time Harvard professor.

Dr. Alpert, frustrated by the purely academic approach of educational institutions to psychology and the healing of people's mental and emotional wounds, became a sojourner and a seeker of spiritual truth among the Eastern religious traditions of Buddhism and Hinduism in India. The process of becoming Ram Dass was truly initiated when his Indian guru, Mahraj-ji, assigned Dr. Alpert to the tutelage of Hari Dass Baba, a silent teacher who used only a blackboard to present lessons that required words.

When Ram Dass returned to the United States, he was on a path that would remain his passion and his vocation. He continued to seek instruction in various forms of meditation, founded several spiritual organizations, and became a teacher and lecturer to help other people find deeper meaning in their lives.

In an article published in *Psychology Today* in March of 1992, an interviewer asked Ram Dass if he thought of himself as a "religious leader":

> I think of myself as a mouthpiece for a process that a lot of people are going through ... I don't look at my audiences as if I know and they don't, because it is not true.
>
> There was a little old woman, about seventy, sitting in the front row of one of my lectures. She wore a little hat with strawberries and cherries on it, a black patent-leather bag and oxford shoes. The audience was all flower children. I thought somebody brought their grandmother. I would tell a far-out story, I would look over, and she would be nodding yes. So I would get a little more outrageous, testing my limits, and she kept nodding. I thought maybe she had a neck problem. At the end, I egged her to come up, and I said, "What have you done in your life to where you know this stuff to be true?" She leaned forward, very conspiratorially, and said, "I crochet."
>
> It blew my mind. Up to then, it was "you meditate in Burma sitting on the full moon on your head after fasting." And she *crochets*. I finally realized that there are lots of routes up the mountain.

IN THE PRESENT

Be Here Now. This is the mantralike title of the best-selling book written by Ram Dass. It is one of the goals of meditation. It is also one of the challenges of daily life.

Being "in the moment" is a skill we need to keep our focus. If we're working, for example, to complete an office project, being in the moment helps us disregard the peripheral issues that distract us from getting the work done. Or if we're trying to pay the bills or write a paper, being in the moment helps us set aside the questions of a confusing relationship for a time in order to complete the task at hand. Being focused helps us listen more deeply to our children, find the clarity to work out a relationship conflict, or enjoy the activity of the moment more fully. Unfortunately, being focused does not come naturally to most of us.

The discipline of meditation can help us find our way to a place where we can be "in the moment." Almost all the world's major religions embrace some form of meditative practice, and some have more than one. From the fingering of Catholic rosaries and the recitations of the specific prayers that each bead represents, to the dizzying twirling of Islam's Sufi dervishes, the world's peoples, whether with great stillness or ecstatic movement, have discovered ways to practice "being present." The reasons to meditate are as varied as the traditions from which they come, but across cultures, meditation is used to strengthen compassion, open-mindedness, and tolerance, to keep useless thoughts and thoughtless actions at bay.

New research shows that meditation also has health benefits. In her book *Zen and the Art of Knitting*, Bernadette Murphy writes, "A number of studies have shown the benefits of meditation. One such study showed that meditation helps reverse heart disease, that it reduces pain, and enhances one's immune system, enabling it to better fight disease. With a group of cancer patients who were taught to meditate, for instance, a different study showed that meditation increases energy while reducing depression, anxiety, anger, confusion, and heart and gastrointestinal problems."

Meditation can also help us relax. In a *Psychology Today* article published in 2001, Dr. Herbert Benson, a cardiologist and founder of the Mind/Body Medical Institute at Harvard Medical School, describes how he began noticing that his patients had elevated blood pressure during routine exams. He wondered if stress could be the cause and set out to test his hypothesis. While the study was underway, Dr. Benson was approached by some practitioners of transcendental meditation who believed that meditation was lowering their blood pressure and wanted him to monitor this. Dr. Benson and a colleague, Robert Keiter Wallace, agreed to check their blood pressure and other vital signs. No similar study had ever been done before, and they were "astounded" by the results. The effect was what Benson called the "relaxation response": "a physical state of deep rest that changes the physical and emotional responses to stress."

If you have ever thought of your crocheting as meditation and then brushed aside the thought, you may be surprised by the results of Dr. Benson's further experiments. He went on to discover that "the relaxation response can be elicited by a number of meditative techniques, such as diaphragmatic breathing, repetitive prayer, qi gong, yoga, progressive muscle relaxation, jogging—even knitting."

Yes, he said knitting, but we can infer—by both the familial relationship of crochet to knitting and by our own experiences— that he would include crochet if he knew of its charms! When we begin to understand that meditation, a practice once thought of as exotic and beyond our reach, is not only accessible and beneficial but also closely related to many of our everyday rhythmic activities, the idea of crochet as meditation takes on a new dimension.

CROCHET IN THE MEDITATION MIX

The basic idea of meditation is to focus on a repetitive sound or motion while putting aside each thought that rises to the surface. The simplest form of meditation that I know of is this:

- Sit in a comfortable position in a quiet place (preferably with a straight yet relaxed spine).

- Focus on your breathing pattern, in and out, and your chest, rising and falling.

- As thoughts come, set them aside. Do not allow them to hold your attention or lead you to further thoughts. Each time your mind begins to wander, return to focus on your breathing.

This practice can be performed almost any place, any time. You can do it for a length of time that suits your needs—just a few minutes, half an hour, or longer. Additional steps might include taking some time before you start your focus to make sure all your muscles are relaxed. You can also choose a sound, a meaningful word, or a prayer to speak or think silently as you exhale each breath.

Now, try it with crochet. Sit in a comfortable spot with your crochet in hand, breathing evenly and setting aside any renegade thoughts. Though meditation practitioners usually close their eyes to avoid outside stimulation, you will need to keep your eyes open to crochet. But you can incorporate short periods of time when you stop for a moment and close your eyes.

You might also want to try a simple form of "insight meditation," during which your focus is on the sensory qualities of your yarn, its weight and texture, its color and feel. Be aware of the movement of your hands, of the flow of the motion. Don't think about what you are experiencing; just allow yourself to experience it. There are no hard and fast rules. Experiment with what works for you.

In her book *Knitting into the Mystery*, Susan Jorgenson makes a statement that captures the essence of this link between the work of our hands and the meditations of our hearts: "Contemplative activity leads us into a complete engagement with two worlds—the seen and the unseen, the material and the spiritual, the world of time and place and the world that knows no time and has no limits."

My personal experience is that the rhythm of crocheting alone can bring on a meditative calm, along with a sense of timelessness and contentment. Just by continuing the rhythm of my stitching, I often find that my thoughts shift from negative energy, brought on by everyday frustrations, to more positive energy. I can also intentionally deepen the experience by setting aside random thoughts and relaxing my muscles. While breathing meditations alone might bring me to a similar place, I find that with crochet in hand, I experience not only the relaxation of the rhythm but also the energy of the yarn's color, texture, and warmth. For me, crochet is very compatible with spiritual dialogue. The richness of crochet, combined with the relaxation and focus of meditation, opens space for the Divine in my mind and spirit.

I believe it is also possible that our tactile connections to yarns and the fabrics made from them have a positive effect on our psyche, though I have not found any research on the subject. Our human need for warmth is one that we all know but tend to forget. Maybe there is a good reason why so many crocheters choose to make baby blankets and afghans! I believe that the spreading warmth of a growing crochet project in our lap brings comfort and healing counsel to both the crocheter and the recipient.

A good project for crochet meditation is to work a square in 100 percent untreated wool. Use a color that you feel particularly drawn to and then crochet it in a basic stitch for your meditation practice. (These simple squares lend themselves to felting projects that you can do later, so you might want to choose a hook a few sizes larger than you would normally use and work your crochet fabric loosely. Suggestions for felting projects are given at the end of the chapter.) The simplicity of working with one stitch makes this a fine vehicle to use to center yourself. By repeating the basic rhythm of crocheting, you physically enact the basic steps of a meditation practice.

Crocheting this project as a meditation has another benefit. When you buy yarn for your crochet meditation, you don't need to have any stitch pattern or completed project in mind. No gauge is necessary and almost any amount of yardage will do. You can choose your yarn colors purely for enjoyment.

You might want to choose a skein each of several different colors and then, when you are ready for meditative crocheting, pick up whichever color pleases you at the time, whether it is a soothing color or an exciting one. This added factor of crocheting with just the right color truly places your crochet meditation "in the moment."

COLOR AND LIGHT

One of the sensory pleasures of crochet is the color of the yarn, though we rarely think about the meanings of specific colors when we choose a beautiful, bundled strand. We usually choose what our pattern calls for or what attracts us at the time. Most of us have consistent favorites because of our personal associations with them, though we may develop an attraction to colors in our mature years that were too intense for us when we were younger.

We are also drawn to different colors and color combinations at different seasons of the year. In the fall, we may find ourselves picking up a rust-red skein, holding it up against a gold-brown without even consciously thinking about the changing colors of leaves outside. We may naturally choose the muted colors of snowy white, cloud gray, and night black in winter; the emerging colors of sky blue, sun yellow, and flower pink in spring; lively splashes of primary red, deep water blue, and leafy green in the summer. The seasonal hues naturally spill into our color choices.

From ancient times, people have ascribed various meanings to specific colors. Across time and many cultures, colors have attained collective associations. For example, red has represented life from as early as Neolithic times, when people were buried with red ochre pigments, presumably to ensure the deceased an afterlife. I have listed some other common color attributes that might add to your enjoyment in choosing colors for your crochet projects—especially projects you are going to create to consciously assist in meditation.

- Red: Red is a high-energy color. It is suggestive of power and prosperity, and it can represent blood and fire. The color red can warm us or raise our spirits when we are feeling low.

- Orange: Orange is connected to the emotions of joy and happiness and can also be associated with creativity. Like red, orange can have a warming effect. It is also believed to aid digestion.

- Yellow: Related to gold, yellow is the color of intelligence and wisdom. It is said to lessen depression and enhance energy.

- Green: The color of growing things, green can make us feel balanced and calm. It has soothing and healing qualities. In spiritual terms, it is green, not red, that is associated with love.

- Blue: Blue is a serene and harmonious color that can have a cooling effect. Think of blue waters over tropical sand. Blue is generally associated with healing and holistic ideas. In ancient Egypt it was considered a divine color.

- Purple: Associated with spirituality and spiritual insight, purple suggests intuitiveness.

- Violet: Violet is the color of peace and awakening to consciousness. Violet in our environment can increase our sense of balance and have a purifying effect.

Another factor that influences our color choice is the quality of light outside—the condition of the sky and strength of the sunlight. Think of the white blouses embellished with bright embroidery so common in Mexico and Central America. Then picture the darker, more shaded tones found in New England textile art. It makes sense that people who live in hot, sunny climates would be attracted to and wear colors that reflect the sun's rays, while people in colder climes would be fond of colors that absorb the warmth.

A little knowledge of how light interacts with crocheted fibers can help us hone our color choices. Patricia Lambert, author of *Color and Fiber*, writes that "yarns in a woven structure … make a lighter, brighter cloth than yarns in a less highly oriented, looped structure such as knitting or crochet." Knowing how the highly textured nature of crochet casts more stitch shadows, we might choose to work with colors of yarn that are a tad lighter than we want our finished fabrics to be. For some projects, we might want to use yarns with a shinier fiber, such as silk, blended in to capture light. Lambert also suggests that light can be pulled into crochet work by "using two or more threads or yarns as one." An easy way to do this is to crochet with two strands from the same color family, the second being one or two tones lighter than the first. (This is where making a swatch before you start your project can help; you can see what effect your color and density of stitch pattern will have on the quality of its light.)

Equally important in our consideration of the light in our projects, is the light within us. I love a statement that the artist Henri Matisse once made about color and light: "It is with color that you render light, though you must also feel this light, have it within yourself." Quakers have a phrase they use to express their care for someone: "I will hold you in the Light." It is a way of praying without words. Historically, Quakers rejected the arts as distracting, but that is slowly changing. For me, the light that plays on form and renders color is one with the light by which we see spiritually. Perhaps you have had this experience when you looked at a great painting that captures light in a beautiful way. Think of the meaning that certain painting holds for you, and you will have a hint of the link between physical and spiritual light.

MEDITATION TURNED INTO PRAYER

A young woman sits on an old bedstead. One leg is bent before her and the other drapes over the edge of the bed where her foot keeps faith with the floor. Her foremost strands of medium long, brown hair are tucked behind her ears, and all the others fall plumb as her head bends forward. One hand plies a crochet hook in and out at the edge of her project, and the other acts as a mediator between the skein and the hook.

The young woman would tell you that she is making a vest—a simple one—for a friend. She knows that stretch, in crochet, runs in the opposite direction than it does for knitting, and so the bodice of the vest will have the gift of "give." Wide straps will be shaped up over the bust, and then narrow and end in button closures at the back. She has discovered how easy and fun it is to crochet ruffles, so the straps of the vest will be softly ruffled at the shoulders.

This picture seems quite clear to me today, as though I have been able to step out of my body and observe myself as a young adult. At that time, I had already discovered the peace that comes with crocheting. I knew that feelings of balance and well-being would come over me as I hooked each new stitch into the stitch below. The repetition of movement and the slow growth of the form in my hands were relaxing and meditative. Yet, as I crocheted that first gift for a friend, something new transpired.

My friend seemed to be present. Memories of shared conversations, gatherings with mutual friends, laughter, even hopes for the future seemed to rise with the rhythm of the work. It was a joyful experience. Love was present not only in my intention to make a gift, but also in the whole process, stitch by stitch. Good thoughts and well wishes formed along my strand of yarn and became part of the web of that vest.

The simple act of crocheting a gift for my friend opened doors to new dimensions of crochet experience. As that vest took shape, the meditative process opened to feelings of love, which in turn became a barely conscious petition for the health and happiness of my friend and for our ongoing friendship. Petition is one of the most common forms of prayer, and though my petition was neither specifically addressed to God nor clearly composed, it assumed the form of a prayerful attitude. From the quieting of my mind, through loving thoughts, to the tentative reaching toward universal love, my meditative crocheting had metamorphosed into prayer.

A new movement is growing in the United States and around the globe that honors the spiritual nature of turning yarn into prayer forms. Meditative quiet and prayer are being hooked and knitted into warm shawls, prayed over, and then given to those needing comfort. Prayer shawl ministries are cropping up in faith communities all over the country.

There are benefits for all who are involved in these ministries. The crafters experience the benefits of prayerful and meditative time at a prayerful and meditative craft. They gather in community with a shared goal in mind, and they help others by passing on a warm shawl—love made visible. The recipients of the shawls feel blessed, knowing that so much love went into their shawl.

When Victoria Cole-Galo and Janet Bristow founded the Prayer Shawl Ministry, neither one of them could have known the proportions their work would take on. Having graduated from the Women's Leadership Institute at Hartford Theological Seminary in Hartford, Connecticut, in 1997, Cole-Galo felt led to knit a special shawl that would be "a gift to [herself] and to others." Listening to leadings that came to her during prayer, she paid extra attention to her stitch pattern, the numbers in her tassel tying, and the attributes of her yarn colors.

When Cole-Galo took her completed shawl to a spiritual gathering at the home of Janet Bristow, who was also a graduate of the Women's Leadership Institute, Bristow "suggested adding beads, charms and trinkets to make it more meaningful." She also suggested "offering prayers and blessings into each stitch and over every shawl."

That first shawl was blessed by everyone present and then given to a mutual friend of both women, who was in need of emotional comfort. The recipient was deeply moved by all the loving care and prayers that had gone into her shawl.

Believing that others might be similarly comforted, Cole-Galo and Bristow decided to create more shawls in the same manner and to concentrate on giving them to new mothers and breast cancer patients. Soon, others around them joined the cause, and word began to spread; the ministry began to evolve and grow, sometimes in unpredictable ways.

I wondered if I could find a prayer shawl ministry in my area. After a few calls and conversations, I finally connected with a priest who had heard about a prayer shawl ministry in a Catholic church about a half hour from my home. The woman who had started the group, Patty, told me the story of their name, "The Emily Prayer Shawl Ministry." Emily, Patty's cousin by marriage, had been a crocheter and a member of the prayer shawl ministry at Emanuel Lutheran Church in Manchester, Connecticut, not far from Vicki Cole-Galo and Janet Bristow's original prayer shawl group. When Emily was diagnosed with brain cancer, the group created a prayer shawl for her—a crocheted prayer shawl for a crocheter of prayer shawls. Emily struggled with the cancer as it invaded other organs of her body and eventually lost her battle. After her death, Patty formed a new prayer shawl ministry in Hampton, Virginia.

The Emily Prayer Shawl Ministry meets in the homes of its members, and the day I visited, Patty was hosting the gathering. When I arrived, four women had already set their hands to the task. Marie was crocheting her shawl in a soft, thick yarn, while Charlotte, Renate, and Monique were knitting theirs. Monique's yarn was deep red, and she was working three-stitch bobbles over the entire surface of her shawl. Renate was working with a pink yarn in a slightly open pattern. Charlotte's lap held a charcoal-gray yarn with colored flecks.

As we waited for others to arrive, Patty told me another prayer shawl ministry story. On the home page of the Prayer Shawl Ministry website (www.shawlministry.com), there is a photograph of a woman seated in an overstuffed chair, holding her daughter, with one long shawl wrapped around them both.

Patty told me that the little girl had leukemia, and a local ministry had decided to make a shawl that was long enough to embrace both her and her mother. The child requested that the shawl accompany her to the clinic for her chemotherapy. Wrapped in her mother's arms and the lovingly created and well-blessed shawl, the young girl was able to accept her therapy.

Prayer shawl ministries often keep binders to record the shawls that are made, the people who make them, and the people who receive them. The story of one recipient piqued my interest. I found out that a man named Jim had returned from a vacation with such severe stomach pain that his wife had taken him immediately to the hospital. They found not only a ruptured appendix but also the beginnings of gangrene. When a gorgeous navy blue crocheted shawl was sent to Jim, he gained much comfort. Thankfully, this seventy-eight-year-old man survived his medical trauma.

Before I left the prayer shawl group that day, I heard one more story about a prayer shawl that a group had made for a woman named Carol, who had been diagnosed with breast cancer. The effect of that gift of one shawl initiated another prayer shawl ministry numbering twenty-eight knitters and crocheters at its inception. This story captures some of the power of the Prayer Shawl Ministry and the widespread, impassioned appeal it holds. And it suggests that the work of our hands can be not only meditative tools for ourselves, but also eloquent messages of comfort and prayers for others.

Ram Dass was right when he said that we don't need to travel to a foreign country or seek a distant teacher to find our way up the spiritual mountain. Some of the answers lie at our fingertips, as close as a relaxing crochet project.

MEDITATION MEETS PRAYER QUERIES

Are you better able to be "in the moment" when you crochet? Think of a situation that might have been improved if you had been practicing being "in the moment." What might you have done differently? What do you think the outcome might have been? Can you imagine any particular times in the future when being able to be "in the moment" might be helpful?

Does your faith tradition have a meditative practice? If so, how does it compare with the effect crocheting has on you? How could you incorporate facets of one practice into the other? If your faith tradition does not have a meditative practice, consider ways you could regularly incorporate the meditation exercise described in this chapter into your crocheting.

Have you experienced a physical state of deep rest (the "relaxation response") when you crochet? If not, might it help to work on a simpler or more complex project? Would it help you to crochet outside or in silence when no one else is at home? What might help you set aside disruptive thoughts as you work?

How do you experience the difference between crocheting for yourself and crocheting for someone else?

What might happen if you made something beautiful for someone you are at odds with?

Working in community for the benefit of someone else can be an especially bonding experience. What benefits do you think you would gain from joining or starting a prayer shawl ministry or another similar charitable crochet group?

Prayer Shawl

The stitch pattern for this Prayer Shawl is one that I have admired for a long time. Since it employs a variation of a three-double crochet shell, it fits the suggestion of the Prayer Shawl Ministry to incorporate the symbolic use of the number three in a prayer shawl: body, mind, spirit; Creator, Christ, Spirit; mother, father, child; faith, hope, love. I crocheted my shawl in a light yellow-gold color. For me, the color yellow symbolizes the harvest or, in simpler terms, a gathering in.

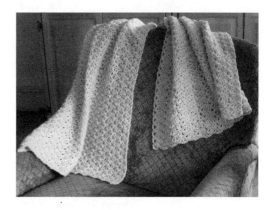

INTENTION

To make a beautifully textured shawl for someone you love or who needs extra comfort. You might also make one for yourself to wrap up in during your meditation or devotional time.

MATERIALS

- about 1,050 yards of soft, worsted weight yarn (I used 5 skeins of Patons Décor.)
- a size K crochet hook (I used a Susan Bates hook.)
- a yarn needle for threading in ends
- scissors

Size: Your finished shawl should be about 24 inches wide, and its length should reach from one outstretched wrist to the other of the person you intend to give it to. If you don't know that measurement, somewhere between 56 inches and 64 inches should work. It may stretch a little in length.

DIRECTIONS

Special shell.

There is one stitch pattern that you will use throughout these directions. Here is how it's worked:

Special Shell: [(1 double crochet, chain 2) twice, 1 double crochet] in the designated stitch.

Chain 86: (You are starting on a short side and working to the required length.)

Row 1: Work 1 single crochet in the second chain from the hook, *skip 2 chains, make special shell in the next chain, skip 2 chains, 1 single crochet in the next chain; repeat from the asterisk to the end, turn (14 shells).

Row 2: Chain 5 (counts as 1 double crochet and 2 chains), 1 double crochet into the first single crochet, skip 1 double crochet, 1 single crochet into the next double crochet (the middle double crochet of the shell in the row below), *work a special shell into the next single crochet, skip 1 double crochet, 1 single crochet into the next double crochet; repeat from asterisk to last single crochet, into last single crochet work (1 double crochet, 2 chains, 1 double crochet), turn. Row two is worked on the right side. You can place a pin or marker on it, or just remember than when the starting tail is on the right, you will be working a number 2 row.

Row 3: Chain 1, make 1 single crochet into the first double crochet, *1 special shell into the next single crochet, skip 1 double cro-

Detail showing the texture of the shawl.

chet, 1 single crochet into the next double crochet; repeat from asterisk to end placing last single crochet into the third chain of the 5 chain at the beginning of the previous row, turn (14 shells).

Repeat rows 2 and 3.

Finishing: Thread in the ends and trim them. You can add fringe if you like or even beads and trinkets, as Janet Bristow suggested to Vicky Cole-Galo. It is mostly important that the shawl be loaded with good thoughts, well-wishes, and prayers.

FURTHER IDEAS

If you have made some squares during your meditation practices, felting them is an excellent way to put them to creative use. You can felt your squares by hand or in a washing machine, using gentle soap and a low level of hot water. (See the felting tips below for more washing machine directions.) You may need to repeat the cycle to get the material to the desired thickness and density. Let your fabric dry flat. Once your fabric is felted, you can cut and sew small projects from it, or cut out pieces of different colored felt to appliqué to other projects. (A good book on the subject is Jane Davis's Felted Crochet.)

Felting Tips

- If you are working with a whole skein of wool, try making your starting chain about 16 inches long. I got nearly perfect 16-inch squares (before felting) when I single crocheted with Brown Sheep Nature Spun (worsted weight), which measures about 245 yards per skein.

- To stabilize larger pieces of fabric and keep the edges from ruffling, fold them in half lengthwise and use an overcast stitch around the open edges with a double strand of cotton crochet thread. Remove the cotton strand when you are finished felting.

- Your fabric will probably shrink more in length than in width.

- If you are using a top-loading machine, set it to hot wash/cold rinse and put it on the lowest water setting. Do not let your fabric go through the spin cycle.

- You can also felt this project in a front-loading washing machine. Place your fabric in a mesh bag or pillowcase large enough that your fabric can lie flat. Set your machine on hot wash/cold rinse. Don't worry about checking it until it has gone through the whole cycle.

- After you cut shapes from your felted fabric, you can give them fuzzy edges by felting them a little more by hand.

- For some simple projects using felted fabric, use cookie cutters as patterns to cut out holiday ornaments. Add embroidery details, plain or fancy, and hang them from a bit of thread.

- Theresa Searle's book *Heartfelt* is a great source for artistic ideas. She has turned the technique of felting into an art form using knitted felted fabrics, but her techniques will also work with crochet. To make a fabric that feels more like a knit fabric, work in single crochet with sport or fingering weight wool.

5
Circles and Cycles
The Art, Meaning, and Use of Mandalas

CENTERING

I gave my love a cherry, that had no stone.
I gave my love a chicken, that had no bone.
I gave my love a ring, that had no end.
I gave my love a baby, there's no cryin'.

How can there be a cherry, that has no stone?
How can there be a chicken, that has no bone?
How can there be a ring, that has no end?
How can there be a baby with no cryin'?

A cherry when it's bloomin', it has no stone.
A chicken when it's pippin' [the egg], it has no bone.
A ring when it's rollin', it has no end.
A baby when it's sleepin', there's no cryin'.

This old, traditional puzzle song was my daughter's favorite lullaby. I loved it as much as she did. It has a sweet, simple melody and familiar images, and the puzzle part is also playful. But I didn't realize until recently the simple beauty embedded in these images of cycles, and the continuity they represent.

Within the short cycle of the song lyrics, a cherry tree blooms, bears fruit, and releases its seed to take root and become another cherry-bearing tree. Chickens and eggs follow each other in infinite succession. Day and night, slumber and light, seasons and years follow babies to their adult awakening. Then comes the begetting of new love, new babies, and new songs. Through all these cycles, the center, the life force of creation, remains.

This concept of the concentric circles of life is central to the sacred art of the mandala. Concentric fields within a mandala may represent the many layers of the procession of time: birth and death, day and night, the cycling of the seasons. Or they may represent the layers of growth that a practitioner must pass through to reach enlightenment.

The basic mandala starts with a circle and a designated center. If we look at many organic bodies, we immediately recognize this circular form with a center: galaxies, solar systems, planets, Earth, atoms, the heads of flowers, the growth rings on trees, fruit sliced horizontally through the center, even the irises and pupils of our own eyes—all are mandala forms.

Mandalas may also feature cardinal points that stand for north, south, east, and west; or forward, backward, heavenward, and earthward; or the four seasons. Though many mandalas have some kind of fourfold construct within, some are free-form and have no points at all. Other mandalas, both old and new, have multiple cardinal points. Rose windows, for example, often have eight or twelve, and mandalas such as those with flower petal motifs or interlocking triangles may have many points.

In Eastern religious traditions, mandalas have a rich and complex history of being created and used as a device for meditation and contemplation. There can be many layers of meaning and highly detailed representations of people, animals, natural phenomena, and cosmic structures present in a mandala. Simple mandalas may be as spare as line-drawn circles or symbols within circles, or they can be highly detailed works of art that are loaded with symbolism and structured on symmetry.

The Western world is less well known for its mandala traditions, yet there are beautiful examples from the past and new, ever-evolving models of mandala art in Europe and North America. Hildegard of Bingen (1098–1179), a Benedictine nun known for her spiritual writings and her musical meditations, painted many mandalas. One such painting is of a circle of trees, cycling through the seasons with their roots grounded at the mandala's center and their branches reaching toward the outer, cosmic edge of the circle.

Cathedral rose windows are an architectural form of mandala found throughout the Western world.

The Navajo Indians of the American Southwest have a mandala sand painting tradition that in many ways parallels that of the Tibetan sand mandala tradition. Specific to the Navajo tradition, the four quadrants can represent the four sacred mountains or the four qualities of light during the four quadrants of the day.

Mandala is a Sanskrit word that means "circle"; its root word, *manda*, means "essence" and *la*, "container." So a mandala is a circle that contains an essence of beauty and harmony, of life and wholeness. Many crocheters and crochet designers are unaware of their historic connections to mandalas, but consider this: are not doilies mandalas? When we choose a doily pattern, we often choose symbols that hold meaning for us: a pineapple pattern for hospitality, a floral pattern to express our connection to nature and our love of beauty, or lacy scallops as a reminder of the feminine. My favorite doily pattern, available through Simple Elegance by Leisure Arts, reminds me of cathedral rose windows. It is called "Anna" and was designed by Patricia Kristoffersen.

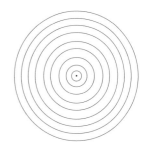

Bindu Mandala.

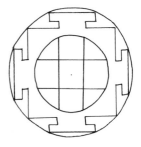

Simple Composite Mandala.

Sri Yantra Mandala.

No matter the style, when mandalas are used as a focal point in meditation, the seeker can find a reflection of the deepest place of the soul in the very center. We can come to the still point that is the "now" of each moment. Our circular crocheted works can become tangible tools to aid our own centering spiritual practice.

MANDALAS FOR HEALING

A particular practice using mandalas has arisen out of the work of Swiss psychiatrist Carl Gustav Jung (1875–1961). During a period of personal upheaval, he began to sketch and paint mandalas in an effort to comfort his own psyche. Sometimes the mandalas he created came to him in dreams, and sometimes he drew them by intuition. Over time, he came to understand that his mandalas represented the state of his psychological health. As his inner fragmentation healed, he could see a record of his process in these small visual metaphors of his inner life. Jung later began suggesting that his patients create mandalas as an aid in their healing.

Eighteen years after Jung's death, a new way of using mandalas as a healing art began to emerge in the United States. In 1979, classically trained artist Judith Cornell had a powerful mystical experience of being "flooded with divine light." In response, she began to paint circular designs with luminescent qualities that reflected her spiritual experience. It would be several years before she learned that her "luminous circles" were actually mandalas.

In 1981, Cornell was diagnosed with breast cancer. Recognizing that fear and other negative emotional reactions might slow her recovery, she used her mandalas and her luminescent art as a catalyst to heal her psyche while allowing modern medicine to work on her body. Now, a doctor of art and philosophy, Cornell presents workshops based on her book *Mandala: Luminous Symbols for Healing*.

Dr. Cornell's workshops, which she offers free of charge to patients at her local cancer center, usually begin with a blessing on the drawing paper and pencils that people will be using and a short introduction to "shading," which is my misnomer, as she uses white pencils on black paper. Participants trace the forms of their hands inside large circles and then illuminate them by creating a "scale of light" with the white pencils. They come away with a personal work of art that is a concrete expression of their spiritual essence and their connection to the light. Many experience the power of this connection as a catalyst to their healing.

These understandings of the mandala as a tool for personal integration and psychological healing suggest that the mandala is an effective vehicle for self-discovery. We can use a circle to center ourselves, to understand who we are, and to find our own wholeness. As Joseph Campbell, the author of *The Power of Myth*, expressed, "Making a mandala is a discipline for pulling all those scattered aspects of your life together, for finding a center and ordering yourself to it."

Today, mandala creation is being used as a tool for meditation, personal growth, and expression in many arenas—ranging from Susanne Fincher's work in art therapy and her book, *Creating Mandalas*, to Buckminster Fuller's geodesic dome structures; to the Mandala Project's online efforts to display a cyberquilt of mandalas.

Brainchild—or maybe I should say "heartchild"—of Lori Bailey Cunningham, the Mandala Project is a unique display of the diversity of humanity in an online gallery. Everyone who visits is invited to submit a mandala, and the site includes beautiful work from many different countries. Through this project, Cunningham hopes that, "Honoring what we have in common while respecting our differences increases our capacity for creating peace." If you want to see this visual expression of healing for the world, check out the website (www.mandalaproject.org). These beautiful and interesting circle designs speak volumes about our unity within our diversity and the vastly creative diversity within humanity.

The Mandala Project makes me think of all the crocheted afghan block patterns I have seen with central mandala-like circular motifs. When worked in individual color schemes and pattern variations, these motifs could be the building blocks of a friendship afghan for a crochet group or even a far-flung group of crochet friends. You could incorporate many pattern designs, or just choose one design and ask individuals to contribute color and texture variations. One of my favorite blocks with a circular center is "Spinner" in Jan Eaton's book *200 Crochet Blocks for Blankets, Throws and Afghans*. With its densely stitched double crochets, "Spinner" would make a warm, draft-resistant blanket. For a more open look, consider "Big Round" from the same book. The central motif looks like a round granny square. When assembled, your afghan will be a wonderful representation of who each contributor is individually, and how richly colored and textured you are together.

FREE-FORM CROCHETED MANDALAS

Curious about whether anyone had linked the spiritual aspects of mandalas and their experiences with crochet, I searched for "crocheted mandalas" on the Internet. My curiosity was piqued when my eyes landed on "What's Cluttering My Couch?" I clicked on the link and reached the online abode of Heather Cox. There to greet me were several photographs of her colorful mandalas, crocheted in a free-form technique and attached to metal rings, with this statement: "I make mandalas from free-form crochet as a meditative/spiritual practice."

One mandala sang a chromatic theme with variations only in the textures of the yarn. Little glassy beads were nested in among the rows of fuzzy yarn. An arc of blue, horizon-like, split another mandala into half circles. The upper half was worked in earth tones, while the blue one below was reminiscent of water. In yet another mandala, a rose, settled at the rim rather than the center, acted as the focal point. Heather's mandalas are quite varied and her approach to making them is unusual. To see them for yourself, and perhaps garner inspiration to make your crocheted mandalas, go to http://clutteringmycouch.wordpress.com/mandala-gallery.

When I contacted Heather to see if she would be willing to share some of her thoughts on making crocheted mandalas, she wrote back saying, "I've been fascinated with mandalas for several years. It's always fun to share with someone. I'm by no means an expert, but I can share what I do know."

Before I start on a mandala, I usually have an idea, or at the very least, a color or yarn I'd like to use. As much as possible, I use yarns I already have. (I don't buy new yarn unless there's something really juicy in the yarn shop bargain bin!) Part of the challenge and the fun is to be creative with what I already have.

From there, my mandalas evolve without much planning. I just see what happens. I use my intuition in every step of the process, from choosing yarns and beads and embellishments and colors to the actual crocheting itself. I work from the center outward, not only because it's the easiest way but also because it's symbolic of being spiritually centered. It's like being at the center of a labyrinth (another spiritual practice I've been fascinated with), which represents the seat of the soul and our connection to the Divine, and then working back out into the world again. Occasionally, I've worked a mandala from a different direction, if it feels right. There was one that began with a golden rose at the top and then radiated out and around and down, like the rays from the sun. It just begged to be worked that way, and I really enjoyed it.

A lot of my influences come from the natural world and from my dreams, from stories and myth. I've been influenced by Carl Jung's mandala concept (which was influenced by Eastern spirituality, of course) as a symbol of wholeness and healing, of the Self. I am very aware of color and healing as I work, especially if I'm making a mandala for someone who's given me a specific request.

Creating mandalas is something that helps me feel more together when I'm feeling fragmented or scattered. I don't think much about what I'm doing. That's the point of meditation, to get out of my head and just be there with the creative process itself. If I'm too much in my head and can't get past that when I start on a mandala, I'll put it away and do some other form of meditation (sitting meditation, walking meditation outdoors) instead and come back to it later.

With mandalas, the calm I get is a quiet state of mind or a quiet state of emotions. It's like a lake without any waves or ripples, smooth water.

MANDALA ART

If you heard someone describe a crocheter as someone who "makes circles that will set your heart on fire!" wouldn't you want to see what they were talking about? That's exactly the description that one person gave Xenobia Bailey's fiber art. After formal studies in ethnomusicology, costume design, and industrial design, Bailey began to pursue needle arts. Her teachers in this endeavor were not university professors but women who had honed their craft. She learned to crochet when she was a CEDA art instructor at The Greenpoint Cultural Society in Brooklyn. There she met Bernadette Sanoma, who told her wonderful stories while she taught Bailey how to crochet—stories of how she learned to crochet from the orphan girls who lived in the convent that was near the elite Italian/Swiss boarding school she attended. Bernadette would have a profound influence on Bailey's life. Bailey learned everything she could teach her, and because she had never been exposed to patterns, Bailey learned without them. "This way," Bernadette told her, "you can create whatever you want."

The long title of Bailey's best-known installation is "Paradise under Reconstruction in the Aesthetic of Funk" or for short, a "Patch of Paradise." As one ArtNet.com reviewer describes it, "Bailey takes the slow, contemplative craft of crochet and pushes it to sensory-packed extremes with great ease and technical control. There are moments of restraint, and moments of concerted, soulful excess." Using only domestic tools, yarn, and a crochet hook, she expresses not only the vibrancy of an inner culture but also the mystery of the universe through large cosmic mandalas.

Bailey's work "Sister Paradise" comes with its own myth: a goddess who sets out to find her lost people, allows herself to become enslaved with them, and then magically spirits them back to their homeland. "Sister Paradise" is a black fashion mannequin in an angelic robe that is replete with rows of bright checks, stripes, and decorative spirals. Her corona resembles the rising sun with small red and white mandalas at each side and red tassels that fall nearly to the floor.

Xenobia Bailey, *Sun Birthing* (stages of the birth of a new sun), 2000. 4-ply acrylic and cotton yarn, plastic pony beads, crochet on cotton canvas backing. 7 x 6 x 8 in. Collection of the artist.

On the wall, setting the stage for this incarnation of soul, are mandalas, many mandalas—clusters of crocheted circles, entire cosmos of concentric rings of color. Many rings of bright colors are cut with rings in neutral colors: white and black. Some mandalas are simple affairs worked only in two colors. Others are rainbowlike, moving into and out of the center. One is reminiscent of the moon. Still others are framed by rows of little gold triangles: I can't help thinking of sunflowers. A very large and colorful mandala hangs alone; an invitation to wonderment. One grouping is comprised of twenty-nine separate mandalas sewn into strategic, eye-catching positions in relation to each other.

If Xenobia Bailey's intention is to bring back a bit of lost paradise, she has more than accomplished her goal. She has brought back whole galaxies, albeit small ones, in concentric rings of color and pattern, mandalas that stir a sense of cosmic sensibility. Though fiber is not her only medium, Bailey has given crocheters, as well as the black community, a glimpse of paradise, a visual expression of something deeply spiritual. (You can learn more about Xenobia Bailey at xenba.blogspot.com.)

MEDITATIVE JEWELRY

Using an innovative technique she calls overlay crochet, Melody MacDuffee is another artist who has made a major contribution to our craft. MacDuffee produces dazzling pieces of mandala-like jewelry that have unique patterns of tiny thread cables laid over the foundation of regular stitches. These miniscule motifs in constantly changing colors delight the eye and lift the spirit. Though MacDuffee did not set out to make a spiritual statement, a sense of the spiritual comes through her work. As she describes it in the introduction to *Crochet Overlay Jewelry,* she started out with thread, hook, and "utter awe" over "the jewel-toned radiance of stained-glass windows; the detailed intricacies of Buddhist sand mandalas; the exquisite, repetitive symmetry of Islamic mosaics and tiles; and the refracted glories one glimpses through a kaleidoscope's lenses."

The spiritual sensibilities that are visually present in MacDuffee's work led me to contact her. I was curious about the inner workings of a woman whose outer gifts conveyed such spirit, and this is what I learned:

I always start with a vision, though often only a vague one. Sometimes it is triggered by a glimpse of something beautiful: hand-painted Islamic tiles, a piece of Mexican embroidery, a radiant stained-glass window. It invariably has to do with some combination of colors that is pulling at me: the way certain hues subtly fade into each other, lulling the eye; the way others stand out against each other, causing each other to pop out visually. Sometimes there's a sense of some evocative shape I want to work into the piece as well. And always there's a desire for symmetry, for balance, for the hypnotic, meditative effect of repeated patterns.

In every case, the "vision" is accompanied by an irresistible compulsion to sit down and realize it artistically ... right now. But the way the piece develops from that point on has very little to do with me, and even less to do with any conception I may have had at the outset. It starts happening, taking on a life—and a direction—of its own. I just lend it my hands and my hook.

This has not always been the case. Having been a verbal, intellectually oriented person most of my life, I had to be dragged scoffing and protesting into the mysterious, ultimately mystical world of letting go. I had to learn that if I wanted to create things that satisfied me, the only control I was going to be allowed to exercise was the offering up of my technical skills to the Universe. I learned the hard way that when I tried to force a piece to conform to my first imaginings, when I tried to think my way to a specific result, it was like banging my left brain against the door to heaven. And the result was always a stilted, unsatisfying thing.

Gradually, I learned that I already owned the key to that door, but that I had to hand it over to some invisible, unpredictable force before it would swing open. I had to give up trying to control the outcome. Later still, I learned to welcome each "error" I made while creating as a godsend, a clue to a more interesting direction to pursue. And I learned to welcome each "accidental" new stitch pattern that spontaneously popped out of me as a reward for having managed to stay out of my own way.

Like meditation, creating for me is a cleansing, refreshing, clarifying process, and for many of the same reasons. On the best days, my mental/spiritual space is clear, capacious, and intensely focused. I "go away" as I create; I lose all sense of time and space and self. When I surface, it is with a sense of awakening, of coming back into the world, but with less stickiness than before. For hours afterward, everything just rolls off me.

Mexican Mandala Necklace by Melody MacDuffee.

MAKING AND USING MANDALAS

Whether consciously or not, crocheters have known the pull of the mandala form since samples of lacy stitch patterns were first layered around each other to become what we know as doilies. Artists such as Heather Cox, Xenobia Bailey, and Melody MacDuffee are leading the way toward new and different crocheted expressions of mandala art. Each of these artists uses a different crochet technique, and each started her mandala project with a different purpose in mind, yet mandala making has become a unique guidepost and a renewing activity in each of their lives. With hooks, thread, willing fingers, and open hearts, others will follow as the seasons and years cycle around.

Though crochet has some limitations when it comes to representing specific figures, it is rich in nonrepresentational potential. Beautiful spiral and circle designs await our hooks and our imaginations. I encourage you to follow your own inspiration, or try the simple mandala pattern of concentric circles at the end of this chapter and personalize it. As you plan your mandala, you might consult the list of color attributes in chapter 4, "Meditation Meets Prayer," or just use colors that speak to you. Consider working in beads and adding charms that hold meaning for you. You might also embroider simple motifs and symbols such as spirals, flowers, and stars onto your completed mandala, or denote cardinal points by sewing beads or small tassels along the outer edge.

Mandala making, as with any other meditative practice, requires some reflective space. Choose a quiet time of the day, a comfortable seat with good light, and create an uncluttered spot for your tools and materials. You might want to put on some soft music or a recording of nature sounds. A scented candle or a little incense adds an aromatic touch. Or consider lighting a plain candle before you begin your work. If you crochet mandalas as a group, you might keep all or part of your gathering time silent, with only whispered interruptions when someone needs assistance.

Lori Bailey Cunningham, founder of the Mandala Project, offers this advice in her book *Mandala: A Journey to the Center*: "The circle becomes a container to hold your most cherished ideas and emotions. You organize your thoughts around a central point that represents a particular theme or concept, and express ideas and meanings by choosing symbols and colors that reflect your intent."

CIRCLES AND CYCLES QUERIES

What are the cycles in your life? How do you, or could you, celebrate them? What is one celebratory ritual you have created that you especially enjoy?

What circle forms in your environment, indoors or out, do you find appealing or restful to look at?

Do you sometimes work projects, not necessarily circular, that are healing for you? What elements of these projects feel healing?

Heather Cox creates her mandalas in free-form. How could you incorporate the free-form method into your crochet? (See the directions for the Scrumbled Tea Steeper in chapter 9 for some ideas on how to proceed.)

Xenobia Bailey's crochet work and her mandalas have stories connected to them. Your crochet projects have stories too, either fiction or nonfiction. One kind of story might simply be the background for one of your projects. For whom did you make it? What patterns and colors did you choose, and why? Did you have any adventures in seeking out your materials? Consider writing down your story.

Melodie MacDuffee tells of learning to let go of expectations while doing intuitive creative work. Think of a time when it became clear to you that you could no longer completely impose your will on your crochet work. What impact did that realization have on your project?

Pocket Mandala

You can make this portable mini-mandala to take along wherever you go. You might slip it inside a book, keep it in a pencil case with a clear front inside a ring binder notebook, or slip it into a photo mailer to keep it clean and flat and take it hiking in your backpack. Or you might prefer to hang your mandala at home where you can see it regularly and take a few moments to focus on its center.

INTENTION

To crochet a simple, portable mandala of concentric circles that can be used as a tool for meditative focus.

MATERIALS

- number 3 perle cotton in 6 colors *(Note: Because perle cotton comes in small, looped skeins, it will be easier to work with if you roll the skeins into balls before starting this project.)*
- When I made this mandala, I chose these colors for their meaning to me:

  Colors 1 and 2: I used two shades of light gold (#677, pale gold and #676, gold) in the center to stand for the warm, loving spirit light.

  Color 3: I used #918, red-brown, to represent the earth.

  Color 4: I switched to #3051, green to represent grass.

  Color 5: I chose #950, pale pink, as the soft, diffused light of a sunrise or a sunset.

  Color 6: I made the outer circle of #823, deep blue, to represent the vessel of the starry universe.

- C or D crochet hook (I used a Boye hook.)
- one marker or knitter's pin (In a pinch you can use a small safety pin.)
- tapestry needle
- sewing scissors

DIRECTIONS

Instructions for changing colors at the end of each round: When there are two loops left on the last single crochet of a round, drop the color you are using and complete the stitch with the new color, then proceed to slip stitch in the chain 1.

Note: You will be working every round in the same direction, raising a chain at the start of each round and making a slip stitch into the chain as you complete each round. Place the marker in the chain at the start of each round.

Color 1

Leaving a 6-inch tail and starting with Color 1, chain 2.

Round 1: Turn, skip 1 chain and single crochet in the chain next to the tail 6 times, slip stitch into the unused chain (6 stitches, do not count the slip stitches).

Round 2: Chain 1, (2 single crochets in each stitch of the round below, slip stitch into the chain) (12 stitches).

Round 3: Chain 1, (2 single crochets in the next stitch, 1 single crochet in the next stitch) 6 times, change to Color 2, slip stitch into the chain (18 stitches).

Color 2

Round 4: Chain 1, (2 single crochets in the next stitch, 1 single crochet in each of the next 2 stitches) 6 times, change back to Color 1 in the last stitch, slip stitch into the chain (24 stitches).

Color 1

Round 5: Chain 1, (2 single crochets in the next stitch, 1 single crochet in each of the next 3 stitches) 6 times, change to Color 2, slip stitch into the chain (30 stitches).

Color 2

Round 6: Chain 1, (2 single crochets in the next stitch, 1 single crochet in each of the next 4 stitches) 6 times, slip stitch in chain (36 stitches).

Round 7: Chain 1, (2 single crochets in the next stitch, 1 single crochet in each of the next 5 stitches) 6 times, change to Color 3, slip stitch into chain (42 stitches).

Color 3

Rounds 8, 9, 10, and 11: Work these rounds in Color 3, making (6, 7, 8, 9) stitches between increases, change to Color 4 in the last single crochet of row 11.

Color 4

Round 12: Work this round in Color 4, making 10 stitches between increases, change to Color 5 at the end of the row.

Color 5

Rounds 13, 14, and 15: Work these rounds in Color 5, making (11, 12, 13) stitches between increases, change to Color 6 at the end of round 15.

Color 6

Round 16: Work the round in Color 6, making 6 random increases.

Round 17: You can either work this round in solid Color 6 and choose to embroider "stars" on it (as noted in the color description), or you can "work in" single crochets every fourth stitch using a contrasting color to create dots. I worked in leftover pale gold from the center of my mandala. To work in the dots: Single crochet the first stitches in Color 6 but yarn over and pull through the last 2 loops with your contrasting thread. Make an incomplete single crochet in the next stitch, yarn over, and pull through the last 2 loops with Color 6. Continue in this manner, making 3 Color 6 single crochets followed by 1 contrasting single crochet. You can carry the contrasting strand either inside the Color 6 stitches or outside along the back.

Round 18: Single crochet around making six random increases, slip stitch into the chain, cut thread and pull through to end off.

Finishing: Gently press your mandala flat by laying it face down on a towel and covering it with a damp cotton cloth. Don't press too hard or too long. Then remove the damp cloth and leave your mandala to dry.

Other Options: Sew a small brass loop to the back to hang your mandala up on a wall hook, or sew your mandala to one or two pieces of quality felt before hanging or allow the felt to act as mats and place your mandala in a simple frame.

FURTHER IDEAS

- Add small charms to your Pocket Mandala that hold meaning for you, or embroider simple motifs and symbols, such as spirals, flowers, or stars. If you like, you can attach beads or small tassels on the outer edge to represent cardinal points.

- Make several mandalas with color variations, hang them together, and either use them for meditation or simply enjoy them for their artistic presence.

- To use a mandala for meditation, hang your mandala so it is a comfortable distance from your eyes. Sit in a straight but not rigid position and look at your mandala with your eyes focused on the center. Try not blink too much, but don't make yourself feel as though you can't blink at all. Your body should be comfortable, your breathing, even. As with basic meditation, try to be in the present moment and let thoughts pass by as they come to you. Let go of worries about what has gone before or what may happen in the future.

• There are two other ways in which you may use your mandala for meditation. One is to follow the circles with your eyes, first working into the center and then back out, a practice that is related to walking a labyrinth. Another meditation used by some Eastern practitioners is to visually memorize a mandala or a series of mandalas.

• If you don't wish to use your mandala as a meditation focus, you might use it just to remind yourself to stay centered and whole or to contemplate other spiritual ideas.

• Make mandalas as gifts to remind friends of the center, the present moment, and of their connection to all that is divine.

6

Prayers on a String

Tools for Intensifying Practice

CREATIVE CONTEMPLATION

Annalee got to leave school early on Friday afternoons, along with two of the boys in our sixth grade class. They all walked downtown for catechism before being released to the freedom of the weekend. I thought that catechism was a kind of Sunday school, but I couldn't understand why it wasn't scheduled for Sunday. Mostly, I envied them their early release from class and their escape outside, especially on warm, sunny Fridays.

When Annalee gathered up her things to leave school, among them was a pretty little book with colorful illustrations and a strand of pink beads that ended in a silver cross. The beads looked like rose quartz. I was interested in gems and minerals at the time, and I owned a set of flash cards, each of which bore a picture of a rock with some information about it. Rose quartz was my favorite, and I loved any jewelry that looked as if it were made with rose quartz. But Annalee never wore her beads. What kind of jewelry was that? When I eventually asked her, she told me that her strand of beads was called a "rosary" and that each bead stood for a prayer she had to memorize and recite. My curiosity temporarily abated. I didn't like memorizing anything—and there were a lot of beads on Annalee's chain!

Though life was pretty concrete in the sixth grade, I did grasp that Annalee's beads could represent prayers and that they were a way to keep God close by. In addition to carrying a rosary and attending "Sunday school" on an odd day of the week, Annalee regularly attended the little stone Catholic church named for St. Ambrose. I attended the Methodist church with my family, but like the other Protestant churches in town, there didn't seem to be anything exotic within—no statuary, no incense, no prayer beads. Yet the core childhood understanding for both Annalee and me was that we were expected to carry the lessons of Sunday service and Sunday school into the ensuing days of the week.

Worshiping in community, following Sunday's teachings during the week, and praying the rosary are all forms of spiritual practice, and they suggest a progression. At the first level, *practice* is used as a noun, and it refers to "the usual way, a custom." This level encompasses various forms of worship, such as the singing of hymns, listening to scripture readings, and reciting the Nicene Creed, as we did in my church.

Practice can also be a verb, meaning "to do," to put into practice. This action-based level includes the ways we live out our faith based on what we sing, read, or recite during church services.

At the third level, the verb form of *practice* means "to rehearse," to do something many times over to gain skill. This kind of practice encompasses memorizing, internalizing, and calling forth prayers and scriptures as we practice being in the Spirit.

With each level of practice, the responsibility of the practitioner grows. At the same time, inner support for the practitioner's spiritual life increases. Each of these forms of practice is important. Merely being present in community can be helpful, bringing comfort to us and to others. Actively carrying spiritual teachings into our daily lives and contributing more of ourselves to the activities of our faith community can increase what we gain from the experience and what we contribute to others. By developing regular habits of reading, prayer, and meditation, we can deepen our faith and broaden our reach for spiritual growth. Practicing our "practice" leads us to meaningful increase in more ways than one.

These definitions of practice can apply to our crochet work as well, when we use it for the purpose of spiritual support. Whether "the usual way" means that we crochet in the company of a group, share tea and handwork with one friend, or ply our hooks in solitude, our mere presence is important. Choosing a regular time to pick up the project we have started, holding the hook, looking at our hands, and appreciating their beauty and ability to serve—these humble actions can contribute to our spiritual well-being.

As we put our crochet skills into the second level of practice, that of action, we learn to trust the rhythmic motions of our hands and, by doing so, create a space in our lives for contemplation. Answers to questions and solutions to problems have an opportunity to rise to the surface. Anger has a chance to abate and compassion, arise. Fear can slink back to its underground burrow and delight can appear when we see that we have transformed our stitches into something beautiful. At the same time, making those stitches can transform us, as we come away refreshed by the time spent in creative contemplation.

If we remember to return regularly to our craft, we experience the third and most common definition of *practice:* repetition to acquire skill. The more we practice, the more likely we are to turn to our hooks and threads to cool our thoughts and clear our minds. Our crochet skills improve, along with our ability to deal with stress. At this level, we open up to the beauty and new possibilities around us.

Our crochet practice will never grow stale if we treat it creatively. You might want to start with a reading, a poem, or a prayer to give you something special to contemplate. Thinking or chanting a mantra (a word that, in essence, means "to free from the mind") can banish thoughts that run in circles and don't solve anything. If you sit tall, breathe evenly, and exhale slightly more than you inhale, you can renew your body while you crochet. Perhaps you will find other ways to enrich your crochet practice, such as listening to music or taking your crochet outside. Meditations from your faith tradition can also personalize your use of crochet as a spiritual practice.

RHYTHMS AND CYCLES

Being reared in a Protestant household, I was aware of the weekly rhythm of services and the yearly round of Holy Days. As I got older, I was intrigued to read about monastic people who practiced the Liturgy of the Hours, and the names Matins, Lauds, Prime, Vespers, and Compline held a certain charm and the romance of a religious culture quite different from my own. The ritual structure of an hourly prayer cycle seemed to hold a sense of security and shared commitment.

In the last few years, I have been introduced to the cycle of spiritual readings created by Rudolf Steiner. When I volunteered at my local Waldorf school, I learned that the sayings written in calligraphy on the pastel watercolored papers decorating the walls were taken from Steiner's *Calendar of the Soul*. Steiner wrote these meditative verses, one for each week of the year, to awaken a feeling of unity with the natural world and to stimulate self-discovery. Later, when I taught kindergarten, I learned that there is a special version of the *Calendar of the Soul* for kindergarten teachers called *In the Light of a Child*. These are simplified weekly sayings, with nods to seasonal changes in the natural world. I saw firsthand how these sayings instilled a sense of wonder and strengthened the inner life of students and teachers alike. Last summer, I took a class in working with very young children, and one of the presenters read a daily reading that I later learned was based on Steiner's interpretation of the Buddhist "right path" precepts (*The Illustrated Buddha Path*).

Hourly, daily, weekly, yearly—across religious boundaries—rhythms and cycles support spiritual life, whether in a monastery, in a school, or in the mainstream of culture. Whether the cycle is the liturgy of the church, weekly sayings, or moment-by-moment mantras, these practices can lead us into the essence of spirituality.

The rhythms with which we order our contemplative time are as important as the rhythm of the practice itself. If we want to use crochet as a contemplative practice, we need to look at the rhythm of our days and the ordinary flow of responsibilities. You might find it more soothing, for example, to crochet for several short periods in a day rather than one longer one. In this case, projects that don't require much shaping or call for any fancy stitches might be best.

If you find yourself using too much of your meditative time gathering your supplies and choosing which project you want to work on, try making a simple blanket on which to spend your contemplative time so you don't have to make a lot of decisions before beginning. Or you might like to work a shawl in a finer yarn than you usually use to extend your ability to focus and find your particular rhythm.

Perhaps you like to make small items and have the satisfaction of completing a project in one sitting. Motifs such as granny squares and crocheted flowers might be just the ticket for you. These projects will give you the freedom to work within the demands of a hectic lifestyle, or to take with you if you travel. The crocheted prayer bead project at the end of this chapter is a good example of a small project that can be completed in one sitting, and you will also have the added satisfaction of being able to use your beads immediately upon completion.

NATURE'S PRAYER SYMBOLS

Prayer beads hold a special place among the various cycles of spiritual life. The history of prayer beads spans many traditions and cultures and goes back further in time than can be documented. Try to imagine living in a time or place where glass and plastic have not yet been invented, precious and semiprecious stones not yet mined. Even if you lived on a major trade route that brought in gems from other places, they were probably too dear for purchase. But you could always find pebbles, shells, seeds, or the bones of small animals.

You might have collected such things to calculate numbers larger than what you could count on your fingers. Or you might have used them as a mnemonic (memory training) device for stories or myths that taught the lessons of your culture and instilled wisdom in those who listened. Perhaps you would have recognized an inherent power in these small items that came from the earth and once belonged to living plants and animals—or were formed in a much earlier cosmic drama. Imbuing these small objects with symbolic spirit would have given them great value and power in your eyes.

You might have moved your talismans from one hand to the other as you recited holy names, presented petitions, decried sins, or told brave deeds. Or you might have laid your objects on the ground in a pattern or dropped them to the ground one at a time while reciting prayers, as Eleanor Wiley and Maggie Oman Shannon describe in their book *A String and a Prayer:* "Records of the third century Desert Mothers and Fathers indicate that they carried in their pockets a specified number of pebbles, which they dropped one by one on the ground as they said each of their prayers."

Eventually, people learned to drill tiny holes in these natural treasures, string them, and reshape them. They began to appreciate them for their visual and tactile beauty and to experience these natural elements for their history. At some point, these strings of stones or shells or, later, beads came to represent the incorporation of the hands into the spiritual life. These small objects became concrete reminders of a bodily connection to Spirit, and people would use them to bless the gifts of the earth. Around the world, many faith traditions developed a practice of tracing some tactile form with fingers while counting prayer cycles, meditating, or remembering scripture.

Hindu Traditions

The sacred beads of Hindus are called *malas*, which in Sanskrit means "garland." For me, the image of a circlet of flowers beautifully expresses the idea of prayers blossoming in a heart place.

It is believed that Hindus were the first to practice prayer with strings of sacred beads. Sandstone carvings that date from the Mauryan Shunga Dynasty (starting in 185 BCE) show human figures holding beads in prayerful gestures. The Hindu *mala*, which consists of 108 beads, is intended to be worn around the neck when not in use by the hands. *Mala* beads usually come from one of two different natural sources. Rudraksha beads are the dried berries of a tree that is found only on the island of Java and are used by those who belong to the branch of Hinduism called Shaivism. The beads used in Vishnuism, the other main branch of Hinduism, are carved from tulsi (a kind of basil) wood. Sandalwood and semiprecious stones have also come to be favored resources for beads.

One strand of *mala* beads provides the structure for several means to prayer and meditation. Each bead can represent the chanting of a mantra. The best-known mantra in the West is the chanting of *om*, the syllable that represents the primordial vibration of the universe and recognizes, on a sound level, that all objects and thoughts are states of energy vibration.

There are other short, intoned mantras called "seed mantras," which can be used by anyone, but in Hinduism, the longer mantra phrases are intended to be given by a guru. Chanting the names of deities, one invocation per bead, is another form of Hindu prayer. With practice, the devotee is cleansed of ego attachments and comes to understand the interconnectedness of all things and the connection of all things to Brahman.

Buddhist Traditions

Taking root in the culture of Hinduism, Buddhism retained the use of the *mala* for fingering while counting mantras and for breathing meditation, but they cultivated different meanings for its use. The count of 108 beads also remained the same, with a "guru" bead placed where the threading ends are joined. In practice, the guru bead is not fingered; rather, practitioners change direction at the guru bead and finger the beads in the reverse direction if they want to continue. A full *mala* is worn around the neck when not in use, while a twenty-seven-bead strand, called a quarter *mala*, can be worn on the wrist.

Each of the 108 beads on the Buddhist *mala* represents a delusion, the most prominent of which is the idea of permanence. Buddhists believe that people are freer and happier if they understand that nothing is permanent, that nothing remains the same, that all things change form—including us. The most common mantra invoked on the beads of the Buddhist *mala* is *"Om mani padme hum,"* which means, "O thou jewel in the Lotus, Hail!" Most believe the jewel to be Avalokiteshvara, the male bodhisattva of compassion. Meditating on this mantra is intended to foster compassion.

Another Buddhist practice is to count off beads while saying or thinking "I take refuge in the Buddha, I take refuge in the Dharma (teaching), I take refuge in the Sangha (the Buddhist community)" for each bead.

Jewish Traditions

Although there is not a prayer bead tradition in Judaism, one tangible object of Jewish spiritual practice is the prayer shawl called the tallit, which has special fringes called *tzitzit* at each of the four corners. In fact, the main purpose of the tallit is to bear the *tzitzit,* in observance of the Torah commandment, "You shall make for yourself twisted cords upon the four corners of your covering, wherewith you cover yourself" (Deut. 22:12).

Tying the *tzitzit* is itself a Jewish art, a form of ritual macramé, and it involves a complex procedure that is filled with religious and numerological significance. A hole is made in each corner, with extra fabric and stitching for reinforcement. Three short strands and one long strand are inserted into each hole, and the longer strand is then wound around the shorter strands a symbolic number of times, with the threads knotted together so the wrappings won't come undone.

There are numerous interpretations for the pattern of these windings. Some believe that the number of windings is related to letter values in Jewish cosmology and that the meaning of these letter values is "God is one." Another interpretation is that each set of windings corresponds to the four letters in God's name. A third interpretation relates to the gematria value of the word *tzitzit*, which is 600. If you add the eight strands (four in each corner, doubled over so eight strands dangle), plus the five knots, the total is 613, which is the number of God's commandments in the Torah.

Regardless of the specific interpretation, the essence of the *tzitzit* is to remind the practioner to be conscious of God's presence and God's commandments at all times. During services, practioners symbolically kiss the *tzitzit* whenever the *tzitzit* are mentioned.

Christian Traditions

The Catholic rosary is the most familiar prayer bead tradition in the West. The word *rosary* is derived from the Latin word *rosarium*, which means "rose garden." As with the Hindu and Buddhist *mala*, this is a reference to being surrounded by flowers, in particular the rose, which has come to represent Mary. The poetry of petals is likened to the inner growth that is experienced with prayer and contemplation.

Most Catholic rosaries contain fifty-nine beads divided into five groups of ten small beads each (called a "decade"), separated by one larger bead at the beginning of each decade. A strand of four more small beads and one large bead with a cross are added at the end of the loop. The beads can be made out of a wide variety of materials, such as wood, glass, stones, or even plastic. One of the more charming traditions is to use beads made of rose petal paste shaped into beads and dried, which retains the scent of roses for many years.

The set of fifty rosary beads also represents one-third of the 150 Psalms, which monastics were required to recite or chant every day, in three groups of fifty, while fingering the beads. A simplified practice for lay people emerged, requiring 150 recitations of the Our Father (a shortened form of the Lord's Prayer). Over time, the prayer cycle has developed into a combination of several recitations, including several Our Fathers, several Hail Mary prayers, the Doxology, and the Apostle's Creed. Celtic Christians, though they worship in ways that are distinct from the Roman Catholic Church, sometimes use a 150-bead rosary that is based on an earlier Catholic form, using the same prayers.

Greek Orthodox and Russian Orthodox prayer strands, unlike *malas* and rosaries, are largely intended for members of the clergy and monastics. Orthodox prayer strands can be made from wooden beads but are most often in the form of a woolen rope with knots to represent prayers. There can be thirty-three, fifty, or one hundred knots in the Greek prayer rope (*metanoia*) and thirty-three, one hundred, or up to three hundred knots in the Russian version (*chokti*). One Jesus Prayer is said for each knot: "Lord Jesus Christ, Son of God, have mercy on me." This recitation is combined with controlled breathing and sometimes with prostrations.

Prayer beads have come to be incorporated increasingly often into Anglican and Episcopalian traditions. In the 1980s a contemplative prayer group created a prototype for a bead strand made of thirty-three beads, to represent the number of years that Jesus lived on Earth. It is divided into four groups of seven beads (called weeks) with four more beads separating the groups. An invitatory bead completes the count, and most Anglican rosaries end in a cross. Perhaps because this tradition is so new, the prayers assigned to these beads have not been codified, though the Jesus Prayer is often used, as well as lines from *The Book of Common Prayer*.

Islamic Traditions

Among the five requirements of the Muslim faith, called the Five Pillars of Islam, is that practitioners stop whatever they are doing five times a day to face Mecca and pray. Prayers are usually completed by saying, "Glory be to God, All praise is due to God, God is most Great" ninety-nine times, while counting the repetitions on the *tasbih*. The word *tasbih* literally means "to praise God" or "to pray to God," and since prayer beads are used in the process of praying, the bead strands have come to be called *tasbih* as well. Each bead represents one of the ninety-nine names or attributes of God—such as Peaceful, Creator, Preserver, the Strong, the Firm, the Unique—and reciting these is a way to worship with the *tasbih*.

Beads for the *tasbih* can be made from a wide variety of materials, such as precious stones, sandalwood, rosewood, or olive wood. Lapis lazuli, a blue stone mined in Afghanistan, is a favorite. Muhammad, the founder of Islam, loved carnelian, a red or brownish-red gem from the quartz family, and he believed that those who wore it would be blessed. Terra-cotta is one of the humbler sources of *tasbih* beads, but these beads become special when they are formed from clay obtained in Mecca or Medina.

NEW WAYS

Many long-held prayer bead traditions have served, and continue to serve, those who adhere to one of the major religions of the world, but not all faith communities have such a practice. As people reach for a spiritual element that they can hold on to, prayer beads are evolving within and beyond formal religious practice. Some religious traditions that had long forgone material aids and ritual are actively pursuing a new vision of the physical connection to the spiritual. There is a growing movement toward an understanding that the body needs to be incorporated into spiritual practices, and some Protestants and Unitarian Universalists, in particular, are developing their own prayer bead traditions.

It is interesting that one Unitarian pastor, James Casebolt, on October 1, 2000, presented a sermon on the world of prayer beads and the benefits of their use, not knowing at the time that another Unitarian pastor, Eric Walker Wickstrom, had already put serious thought into what Unitarian prayer beads might look like, and his ideas had been presented in Scott Alexander's *Everyday Spiritual Practices*.

In another almost simultaneous manifestation, Earth beads were born. In 1999, two Passionist Catholic Sisters "felt drawn to create a special prayer form that individuals could use to focus on the healing of Earth." They began to make blue and green polymer beads and string them into wrist-sized loops that they called Earth Prayer Beads.

A couple of years later, not knowing about these Earth Prayer Beads, a woman named Paula Hendrick designed a set of prayer beads for those attending her Earth Story Circles. Hendrick used beads to symbolize the evolution of Earth, along with shapes to represent stars, birds, turtles, flowers, and crescent moons. She calls her beads Cosmic Rosaries, or Universe Story beads, and believes that in the process of making these beads "everyone learns that our scientific story of the universe is a sacred story." (As a guideline for making your own set of these beads, she offers a sample universe timeline at www.ecovillage510.org/paulaspage.html.)

Other creative approaches to making prayer beads give them more personal meaning. People who take the bold first step of joining Alcoholics Anonymous are immediately encouraged to admit that they are powerless over their addiction, to come to believe that a Higher Power can help, and to turn themselves over to that Power for guidance. Toward that end, a woman named Gwen began to create strands of twelve prayer beads as a reminder of the twelve steps, and to be used specifically in the practice of step 11, which is to seek a deeper relationship with Higher Power through prayer and meditation. (If you'd like to see her beads, visit www.twelvebeads.com.)

Another creative prayer bead maker named Karen has researched traditional prayer beads and makes strands for herself, altering them slightly to fit her needs. She has also made strands that suggest the cycles of the moon and the cycles of the seasons. One of Karen's most endearing ideas is that of a Motel Rosary. She collects the soothing names of motels in favorite vacation spots—such as Fireside, Riverwood, and Silver Moon—and recites them on the beads of an Anglican rosary. For her, "Reciting these names is like going on a mountain retreat." (You can see Karen's prayer beads at www.angelfire.com/my/zelime/beads.html.)

One especially rich source of ideas for making personal prayer beads is the book *A String and a Prayer,* by Eleanor Wiley and Maggie Oman Shannon. They encourage people to use numbers, colors, and materials that hold personal meaning, to add charms and amulets as symbols of character, special knowledge, attainment, or attachment. "In the end," they say, "all prayer beads are about peace—coming to this place within ourselves so that we can be at peace with others."

MEDITATIVE GEMS

As crocheters, we know something about the meditative effect of working with our hands. We have experienced the effect of repetition that takes us to a place where our bodies are relaxed and our minds become still. Beading—stringing one bead at a time into its place on a silken or a humble cord—can have a similar effect. So it seems only instinctive that beads and crochet come together beautifully to bring our heads, hearts, and hands into a wholistic balance. Taking a step from crochet into the realm of crocheted prayer beads is a natural spiritual practice for us.

I like to think of crocheted prayer beads as jewels or meditative gems to be used not for adornment but for a deeper, contemplative purpose. Crocheted prayer beads could represent a specific concept, such as compassion, a generous spirit, or spiritual growth. Or they could represent our connection to the natural world, the wisdom we have gained from our own experience of a natural cycle. Crocheted prayer beads could honor friends, family members, and pets; celebrate babies, birthdays, and passages; provide meditative support for special times of the day.

A crocheted chain to hold beads is soft and fluid and offers a different experience from the clicking of strung beads. Some might ask if a crocheted cord is strong enough. A Buddhist practitioner would respond that nothing is permanent and restringing beads when they need it is a good exercise in understanding impermanence. But gently used beads won't come apart too quickly, and the smooth fibers will be soft against your skin.

As you hook your stitches and slide your beads into place, you may want to let each bead represent a peaceful breath, a mantra, or a favorite line from a prayer or poem. If you are making your prayer beads for a friend, you might want to breathe a blessing on each bead as it is worked into place.

You might enjoy thinking of each bead as a tiny receptacle to hold the meaning you assign to it. Each bead, then, becomes part of a larger cycle that will draw you into a contemplative place each time you finger it. The reverent tone you set to crochet your beads will become part of the reverence you feel as you use your beads. If you think of reverence as a special kind of respect, with overtones of awe and wonder, there is much to revere in our surroundings, our everyday lives, and our creative nature—if we look for it.

PRAYERS ON A STRING QUERIES

What do you understand "spiritual practice" to mean in your faith community? If you are not presently worshiping with a group, how do you imagine a practice that would support your spiritual life?

Making our lives regular and rhythmic can help keep stress at bay. In what ways can you add healthy rhythms to your daily routine with your crochet and other activities?

How do you feel about using rituals and tangible, tactile objects to support your spiritual life? What rituals or practices have been helpful to you in the past?

How do your head, your heart, and your body each play integral parts in your spiritual life?

Almost Universal Prayer Beads

In some traditions, prayer beads are worn; in others, they are simply carried. This crocheted strand of beads can be draped around your neck and then removed for meditation and prayer any time you have a quiet moment to use them.

I have chosen to use thirty-three beads for counting prayers or meditations, with accent beads in between. This number works for various traditions. For Christians, the thirty-three beads can represent the thirty-three years of Jesus's life on Earth. For Greek and Russian Orthodox practitioners, thirty-three is the smallest number used in traditional *metanoia* and *chokti*. Muslims can pray three cycles around the beads, for a complete set of ninety-nine prayers. If you place markers, such as beads of a slightly different texture or small tassels, after the first three beads and before the last three, the central twenty-seven beads will make a quarter *mala,* for Hindus or Buddhists.

I often use my beads for breathing meditation, following breaths in and out while setting aside mental chatter, and sometimes for chants such as *om* (pronounced "aah-ooo-mmmm"). You can use any practice or prayer(s) you like. When you are meditating with prayers, you might try assigning specific prayers to specific beads, or using one prayer that you repeat over and over, or praying one line of a long prayer for each bead.

INTENTION

To make crocheted prayer beads to use as a tactile support for meditation, contemplation, or prayers.

MATERIALS

- 1 skein of worsted weight cotton yarn (quality cotton with sheen is best). (I used Cotton Classic by Tahki, Stacy Charles, Inc.)
- 33 glass pony beads (8 millimeters outside, 4 or 5 millimeters inner diameter)
- 34 smaller pony beads (about 6 millimeters with a large hole)
- 1 large bead to end the loop and sit on top of the tassel
- size G crochet hook (I used a Susan Bates hook.)
- yarn needle that will easily fit through the bead holes (size 16)
- regular sewing needle
- thread that matches your yarn
- scissors

DIRECTIONS

Cotton yarn often comes in a skein or hank. If your yarn has come in a skein, roll it into a ball before starting. You might want to place your ball of yarn in a bowl or box while you work so that it doesn't jump around.

Thread your yarn needle with the starting end of your yarn and slip one small pony bead and then a larger one onto the yarn 33 times, continuing to alternate the smaller pony beads between the larger ones. End with the last small bead.

Push the beads further down the yarn and make a slip knot, leaving an 8-inch tail.

Chain 136.

Turn and slip stitch in the second chain from the hook. Insert the hook in the next chain, slide the small bead down as far as it will go (behind your hook), yarn over, push bead toward you, and complete a slip stitch, slip stitch in the next chain, insert the hook in the next chain, slide a larger pony bead behind the hook and slip stitch it in place. Slip stitch in the next chain.

Pushing the bead toward you will nestle it nicely in the stitch.

Continue to alternate slip stitches and slip stitches with beads until all 67 beads are worked in. End with a slip stitch in the last chain.

End off, leaving an 8-inch tail.

Finishing: Pull one yarn end through the other end of your bead strand to form a loop. Tie the two ends together with an overhand knot. Thread both ends through the large bead. Cut 13 strands of yarn, each 11 inches long. Lay the center of the strands into the two yarn ends hanging below the large bead. Tie the two ends tightly in the center of the cut strands. Pull all the ends down. Now, wrap thread the same color as the yarn tightly around this bundle and about a half-inch below the large bead. Work the thread ends in tightly with a sewing needle. Trim the tassel ends.

FURTHER IDEAS

Now that you know how easy prayer beads are to make, you can personalize your prayer bead strands in a variety of ways.

• Make a wrist-length string of beads.

• Make your crochet strand in a different stitch pattern, or crochet a seed bead spiral on which to incorporate your beads.

• Draw ideas from a variety of traditions, taking into consideration the bead count, the kinds of beads you choose, and the way you intend to practice with your beads.

• Experiment with color. After all, if *rosary* means "rose garden" and *mala* means "garland," why not make prayer beads in a riot of color? What better way to create visual joy than by stringing beads onto a richly hued strand—a strand that isn't hidden inside the holes of beads but clings alongside them? Making crocheted prayer beads is a great opportunity to use yarn and beads that set up a contrast, or materials in several shades of one color that vary in texture. What about crocheting yellow beads onto jade-green yarn, or rose-pink beads onto royal blue? Or crocheting a strand of beads in the regal colors of red, blue, and deep purple onto a gold or silver yarn? Or using gold, silver, white, or black accent beads to brighten or soften the effect of your yarn colors for the yarn and the larger beads? (You might want to check the list of color attributes in chapter 4 for some of the affiliations and meanings of specific colors.)

• Charms, tassels, and special beads can personalize your prayer strand. Fiber tassels are also a natural addition for color, and tassels make a great ending for your prayer loop. If you choose to add tassels, consider making several in differing sizes.

• Make a variety of prayer bead strands, changing them to suit different prayer cycles. You might like to make a strand with just enough beads to accommodate the lines of a particular prayer or a poem that feels especially spiritual to you.

• Make prayer bead strands to share with friends. Include suggestions for how to use the beads with your gift.

• Create a notebook to fill with prayers, poems, and contemplative verses you especially like for use with prayer beads.

7

Pathfinding
Finding Our Way with Crochet

OUR COLLECTIVE HERITAGE

Over many thousands of years, fiber preparation, cloth making, and garment construction and embellishment have been mainly the domain of women. In *Women's Work: The First 20,000 Years*, Elizabeth Wayland Barber explores why the textile crafts have traditionally been so gender specific. One obvious reason was that spinning, weaving, and sewing were necessary tasks that could be accomplished with the least danger to children. They were also "repetitive, easy to pick up at any point, reasonably child-safe, and easily done at home." Barber draws on a 1970 article in *American Anthropologist* in which Judith Brown found that preindustrial communities assigned work to women according to the work's compatibility with raising children. The criteria for such work was that "they do not require rapt concentration, and are relatively dull and repetitive; they are easily interruptible [I see a rueful smile on every caregiver's face!] and easily resumed once interrupted; they do not place the child in potential danger and they do not require the participant to range very far from home." It seems, historically, that women's collective path has been to tend children and hearth fires alike, while creating clothing and other household textiles.

Of course today, with the possible exceptions of mending, hemming, and sewing on buttons, we have no need of fiber skills. All the early facets of fabric manufacture—carding, spinning, weaving, sewing, and eventually knitting—met the whirlpool of the Industrial Revolution, which sucked huge amounts of hand labor into the depths. Yet, some managed to portage around the Industrial Revolution and set their boats afloat again on smoother water. Fiber art and craft did not die once textile manufacture was taken over by machines. In fact, it is ironic that crochet may be the fiber craft most supported by the mass production of thread while, at the same time, being the most difficult to mechanize.

Tree Cozy by Carol Hummel. Sculpture in the Heights Public Art Competition, Heights Arts, Cleveland, OH (juried) Winner 2005.

Now we can pursue the fiber arts for pure enjoyment as well as for practical use. And pure enjoyment it is, in some cases, without one microfiber of practicality. In the December 2006 issue of Dora Ohrenstein's webzine *Crochet Insider*, I was delighted to find the wonderful, whimsical crocheted art of Carol Hummel. Her work titled "Tree Cozy" was a turtleneck sweater for a real tree! The sweater branched in every direction the tree did. In winter, the leafless tree looked warmly and colorfully dressed. In spring, its foliage was a perfect match for its striped wrap.

Maybe you have seen some equally touching and humorous examples of crocheted art. Or perhaps you have had a glimpse of the artistic, one-of-a-kind garments and accessories that are sold in specialty stores. Crocheted jackets, sweaters, and coats too complex to record the instructions for cross the bridge between what is "usable" and what is visually and palpably exciting. Hats, bags, and garments hooked using scrumbling and other free-form techniques dazzle us like the jumbled bits of color that appear with every turn of a kaleidoscope. Maybe you aspire to create these kinds of crocheted wonders yourself.

Whether you crochet to soothe yourself or to make people chuckle, to create beauty or warmly cover the body, or to push the craft to its visual limits, you are already on your own crochet path. For some, the path to vocation and the crochet path will merge. Others will reserve crocheting for "pure enjoyment" and will take a very different road with the craft. Either way, crochet has lessons to teach all of us about staying on track.

We build up our crochet skills little by little, over time, yet sometimes we forget that these changes take place in a series of small increments. Whenever we start a crochet project that will take its final shape only after working many motifs, granny squares, or other modular pieces, we are reminded again of the need to take one step at a time: one stitch, one motif, one section. Even as our fingers and minds shape each integral piece, we internalize this idea. And we learn and relearn that tending carefully to each part of the whole not only provides us with beauty in the moment but also a beautiful finished project. Crochet can remind us to work at our own pace, to nurture our dreams of accomplishment, and to enjoy the journey.

Along the way, we learn to look at things from differing perspectives. When we master a new stitch, we might stop to turn our sample and view the pattern at a different angle. We might see that rows worked horizontally make interesting ribbing when they are turned vertically, which could make a great yoke for a sweater. Maybe we realize that one lace pattern is a nice match with another, and that the two stitch patterns combined would make a fine shawl. In the same way, we need to be able to see life situations from more than one angle, especially when we have to make major decisions. Looking carefully at the things that puzzle us, turning and manipulating ideas, making connections that aren't immediately apparent—these are all lessons that we carry with us from our creative work with crochet into our life work.

We absorb other lessons when we understand how to crochet with gauge. When we make a sample and take a gauge (by measuring the number of stitches per inch and rows per inch), we are checking to see if our hook and yarn size will produce an item in the proportions the pattern designer intended. Testing by making a small sample can keep us from making a big mistake. A similar kind of testing might be very valuable when we make major changes in our lives. If, for example, you are thinking about changing your occupation, you might "sample" the new work environment by requesting an opportunity to observe at the workplace, or volunteering some time to the organization to get a taste of what a formal position might be like. Just as taking a gauge will make a pair of socks or a sweater fit properly, trying things out and gauging their success may help with reaching the next destination on your path.

It is rare that we find our path early in life and then never stray from it. Most of us have, at one time or another, struggled with finding our way. We may be surprised to find that hints, like little clues in a scavenger hunt, can come from our everyday activities, especially the ones we love, such as crocheting.

THE ART OF SEEKING

Craft, spirituality, and vocation all require a certain reaching out, a seeking of inspiration, a search for wisdom. Part of seeking is staying curious, open to possibilities, even energized by the search, carrying with us the faith that what we seek will be found.

The story of George Fox, the founder of the Religious Society of Friends (Quakers), is a story of seekers in more than one sense of the word. Fox, who was born in Leicestershire, England, was reared in the ways of the Church of England in a parish with Puritan leanings. The depth of his interest in all things religious and spiritual suggested to some of his relations that the priesthood might be his path. Instead, he apprenticed to a shoemaker and a grazier. Shoemaking and shepherding suited his contemplative nature, and during the time of his apprenticeship, he started to solidify some of his ideas about humility and simplicity.

Fox had many questions that the Bible and his church couldn't answer for him. Though he conversed with many educated people and clergymen in his search, no one's answers satisfied him. For Fox, seeking meant refusing to settle for answers that didn't strike a deep chord of truth in him. Over time, prayer and meditation led Fox to insights that he called "openings." Because of this, Friends today use the phrase "way opens" to describe insights and opportunities.

In 1652 Fox felt lead to climb to the top of Pendle Hill where he then had a vision of "a great people to be gathered." After descending Pendle Hill, he traveled to a nearby town where there was word of a group of people looking for spiritual truth. On reaching the town, Fox found over a thousand people who were called, quite literally, the Westmorland Seekers. George Fox, the seeker, had found his congregation, and the Seekers had found a leader. Way opened.

Fox's journey tells us something about finding our own paths. It was fortunate that his parents didn't steer him directly into the ministry. Instead, he was given a period in which to work with his hands, to continue to read and question, and to consider what was in his heart and mind. He listened not only to the wisdom of others but also to the whispering of his own conscience and the still, small voice of the Divine.

In my spiritual seeking, I have learned many things from Quakers, not the least of which is the pathfinding language that is integral to the story of George Fox. In Quaker terms, someone who is "seeking" and listening for the "still, small voice" may experience a "leading," the whisper of a suggestion or the gift of an idea previously hidden. The Quaker approach of humility and a quiet spirit is the contemplative foundation for finding our path. Way does often open.

But way doesn't always open conveniently in front of us. Parker Palmer, a contemporary Quaker who has written eloquently on the idea of listening to find our true vocation in life, began his search for vocation as a young adult. An intelligent and energetic man,

Palmer was offered and took several enviable positions, only to meet with failure and frustration. Way had opened but it was not satisfying. In his book *Let Your Life Speak: Listening for the Voice of Vocation*, Palmer explains that it was with laughter and relief that he finally accepted the wisdom of an elder Quaker woman who told him, "I'm a birthright Friend, and in sixty-plus years of living, way has never opened in front of me, but a lot of way has closed behind me and that's had the same guiding effect." When he took his real gifts, sensitivities, and limitations into account, he became a well-known and respected teacher and writer.

For some, a vocation is simply "an occupation, business or trade"; others understand vocation as a calling of a spiritual nature, not as a goal to pursue but a calling to hear. As Palmer puts it, "Before I can tell my life what I want to do with it, I must listen to my life telling me who I am…. Vocation does not come from a voice 'out there' calling me to become something I am not. It comes from a voice 'in here' calling me to be the person I was born to be, to fulfill the original selfhood given me at birth by God."

This statement touches on a core kernel of truth: it is in knowing our true selves that we find our true vocation. This understanding of ourselves is one of the gifts we can uncover through contemplative crochet. We may gain helpful insights into our personality by looking at what patterns and items we choose to crochet and how we go about bringing our projects to life. Are you drawn to patterns that require only skills you already possess, or do you like a gentle challenge? Do you often dive in "head first" for the sake of a glorious outcome, or do you prefer to stick to pattern instructions? Do you combine ideas from several patterns, or would you rather create something totally original? Do you crave whimsy? Are you drawn to beauty? Maybe you express a rebellious streak in your use of images and color. All these things and more express who you are.

The multifaceted nature of our craft can reflect our own nature back to us. Supported by the quiet rhythm of crochet, our inner ears can become attuned to our inner mysteries. We are able to listen for the presence of our true selves, and self-knowledge becomes our axis point. From this center, we can move backward or forward or in any other direction we wish, and we will know exactly where we are. Stitch by stitch, we can uncover our gifts and our limitations, and we can find ways to honor who we are and who we are becoming.

A DANCING PATH

One of the ideas that Parker Palmer suggests in *Let Your Life Speak* is that we each need to face "the 'no' of the way that closes and take the 'yes' of the way that opens and respond with the 'yes' of our lives." For each of us, finding our way on that path is unique. I see my own path as very much like the movements in a circle dance, starting in the center, moving to the periphery, promenading with new partners and then back into the center again, over and over. At the center of my circle is an early love of fabric and fiber. I have a memory, from around the time I was in kindergarten, of trying to cut pieces of red plaid wool and piece them together with electrical tape to make a bathing suit. Well, "bathing suit" was the idea, but as you can probably guess, there was no finished product. With children, process is everything, they say.

On and off, over time, I learned new fiber skills and honed old ones. My mother taught me how to sew and how to knit and purl. Throughout my high school years, I sewed a lot of my own clothes, and I knitted one project—a white ski band in a knit-and-purl seed stitch. It wasn't until the very end of high school that my friend Toddy taught me how to crochet. Later, a friend taught me to spin. With that skill, I made myself a pair of socks from scratch, first spinning the singles, then plying the singles, and finally using a book for young knitters to teach myself how to turn the heels.

The music really began to swing and the dance to form when I tried a cloth-doll-making experiment, incorporating the other fiber skills I already had. I made a dozen or so dolls from Carolee Creations patterns and then started to make my own doll patterns, dressing my small people in original smocked dresses, embroidered playsuits, little sweaters with crocheted trim and booties. There was strength in consolidation, and I went to the center of the circle with an impassioned focus for several years.

With a preschool daughter, upheavals in our lives, and an aversion to selling my dolls to collectors rather than to children, for whom I had designed them, these dolls faded out of my life, and I danced back to the periphery, though I continued to make Waldorf-style dolls for my daughter, Naomi, and paper dolls—seeking something simpler that could be made for children and still be appealing.

When my daughter was junior-high age, I presented a weaving workshop for her and a few friends. The workshop was well received, and I began to wonder about the possibility of doing a sock doll workshop. On the day I went out to buy socks to experiment with, I arrived back home with a bag of socks and a new paradigm, distinctly different from all the folk techniques for making dolls from socks. Sock dolls poured forth. In no time, I understood that I could write down how to make the dolls, share the idea with others—maybe even make some money. Dolls were back in the center again, this time with writing as a companion and a new focus: teaching through publication, in my *Sock Doll Workshop* book.

Focuses can be intense, and when release comes, we need to play again. As I danced around the periphery again, I contemplated this "way opening" of publishing for me. This time, I decided that I would deliberately choose what I wanted to publish next. This time I wanted it to be something that I could see myself doing for the rest of my life. I missed crochet and the way it made me want to create, while also making me feel grounded. I missed daydream designing and the quirky ways to play with color that are inherent in three-color patterns, granny squares, and free-form work. So I chose the craft of crochet. I started a book of crocheted mittens, but no publisher would have it. (Crochet didn't exactly have a healthy market in the last decade of the twentieth century.) I bided my time, designing and marketing individual patterns. Then I began to work on a book for beginners that I felt would set them on a good track as potential designers. I was back in the circle of focus again when a publisher offered me a contract for the manuscript that would become *Single Crochet for Beginners*.

Out to the periphery of the circle I waltzed when that book was sent to the printer. This time, I had only promenaded a short distance around the circumference when I had my own vision of writing a book about handwork and education. Three days into preparations, I received a call asking if I might like to write this book on spirituality and crochet. I was right back into the center of the circle with new partners.

A WALKING PATH

The path of vocation is often an irregular and uncertain one. Sometimes we march boldly across open meadows of surety, at other times we push through dense forests of doubt, and occasionally we stop altogether at a river of dilemma. Then we must find a way to ford the river or turn back. When the way is not clear, when the path is full of obstructions, we need some clues about what to do next. We need some clarity to find our way.

The obstructions in our path aren't always as large as a river or a fallen tree. At times, even a small frustration can keep us from moving forward. Have you ever lost your favorite yarn needle for threading in ends and gone in circles trying to find it, checking multiple times in the places where you were *sure* it must be—on your desk, in your crochet basket, in every project bag—only to finally sit down, calm down, and suddenly remember exactly where you last had it? (The last time I lost my needle, it was in a basket I had taken out for a crochet workshop.) When we give our bodies and our brains a break, we allow our less conscious mind to tell us what we already know at some level.

Most of the time we operate out of our rational, rushing, goal-oriented state of consciousness. We may need to "gear down" to our less conscious selves if we want to listen to a deeper wisdom. Our less conscious mind is as important as our conscious one. It is the ground where we can get in touch with the mysteries that we can't always name or even put into words. It is the field in which creativity and spirituality can sprout and grow.

Connecting to our intuitive and less logical self is another way of knowing who we are and staying on our path. One pathway is through repetitive activities that support a meditative state. When I am using an easy, repetitive crochet project as a meditation practice, I am connecting with my restful, unconscious mind. But if I am designing a crochet project that needs to meet certain criteria, I am working hard with my conscious mind to think about what my options might be. Sometimes it is helpful to switch to the less conscious activity of relaxed crocheting and allow solutions to come to me more freely. Or, I might get up and go for a walk. Moving my body is an active way to invite my less conscious mind to join my conscious mind in seeking a solution. If I let go of my conscious questions altogether and allow the physical rhythm of walking to take over, sometimes the answers come.

When I was working on *Single Crochet for Beginners*, I needed to come up with a small unique project, worked only in single crochet, that beginners could use to experiment with increasing and decreasing and not have much to lose if they made a mistake. The project needed an element of fun, too. One evening, I went out for a walk and as I found my stride, I also found my bow tie project.

A crocheted bow tie.

Walking has long been used as a spiritual practice, formalized most notably in the use of labyrinths. In the twelfth and thirteenth centuries, labyrinths delineated by contrasting colors of stone were laid into the floors of large cathedrals. It is thought that these winding paths, contained within a circle, represented the challenge of finding a path to God. Walking a labyrinth was thought to symbolize a pilgrimage, which could be made by anyone, rich or poor, as long as the person was capable of walking a relatively short distance. In recent years, there has been a resurgence in the use of labyrinths as meditative practice.

A Buddhist approach to walking meditation has also been made readily available to the Western public by Thich Nhat Hanh in his book *Walking Meditation*. He lays out a way to incorporate breathing meditation with slow, meditative walking. The practitioner takes two, three, or four steps for each in-breath and the same for each out-breath, eventually making the out-breath slightly longer to expel all of the old air from the bottom of the lungs.

As a crocheter and a walker, I began to consider how walking as meditative practice could be joined to my crochet practice. It would get me off my personal cushion and into the sunshine to soak up some vitamin D. It would exercise my body, increase my blood flow, and still give me the satisfaction of accomplishing a small amount of handwork.

I experimented with putting my crochet project into a light-weight shoulder bag and wandering up and down in the safety of my driveway, legs in gear and crochet in hand. I realized that I didn't have to coordinate too many things at once; just walk slowly in a safe environment and make one stitch at a time on a small project. It could be done!

Women have long done more than one thing at a time. Walking and working with our hands is not new. In *Women's Work* there is a picture captioned, "Seventeenth century woodcut of women in the Balkans spinning while traveling. Spinning was such a time-consuming yet simple and necessary job that women frequently spun thread while doing other things." (We can only wonder how meditative this scenario actually was!)

One fiber friend told me about seeing a painting, in the background of which a woman was knitting out of her pocket as she walked. Another friend told me a story about the "seven-mile mitten," which has to do with knitters knowing they can complete a specific project in the time it takes to walk from one place to another.

Perhaps you've discovered the amazing work of Marianne Seiman, a crochet artist from Estonia who is gaining recognition. Her work includes free-form garments made from many variations of circle motifs, crocheted bags embellished with add-on crochet and embroidery, and crocheted, felted flower jewelry fit for a garden princess. What's especially interesting to me is that Marianne takes her three children and her crochet motifs out walking. When asked in an interview about her personal style, she replied, "Why are many of my works built up with circle motifs? Because it's something I can do while walking with the kids or looking after them or waiting for the food to cook. It's easy to pick up and put down when needed." Marianne Seiman has found a path that feeds her soul while tending to her family.

Here, I have to admit that doing two things at the same time is not really my style in the long term, but I have found another way to enjoy the meditative effects of both walking and crocheting. I love to take walks, carry my crochet with me, and weave periods of crocheting into my walking. I like to walk for a while and then make myself at home in a pretty spot where I can crochet, think, and gaze at my surroundings. This pattern of walking and crocheting puts me in touch with the earth under my feet, my creative energy, and the energy of all creation.

Fitting activities together for mutual benefit, it seems to me, is a microcosm of our pathfinding mission. We seek activities and goals that we love and can give ourselves over to. We seek a place in our lives for those passions and a place for ourselves in the world. In an ongoing process, we work with our loves and our limitations and take joy in the harmony that comes with a life in balance.

PATHFINDING QUERIES

What gifts and potentialities do you perceive in yourself? Are they being used? If not, what small steps might you take toward using them?

Allow yourself some time to contemplate Parker Palmer's statement, "Discovering vocation [means] accepting the treasure of true self I already possess." Consider the idea that the thing you most want to do is the activity you were meant to do. What effect would embracing this idea have on your life and your vocation?

What means have you sought to deepen your spiritual life and deepen your relationship with your craft?

Think of a circumstance in your life where you searched and searched for answers from others, only to realize that the answers came from somewhere inside you. Have you developed a sense of security that ongoing solutions will emerge in due time?

Have you ever given your conscious mind a break from problem-solving (perhaps via walking, crocheting, or meditating) only to "find" a solution to a problem or have an idea that was very different from the one you originally had in mind? (When I wrote Sock Doll Workshop, I had been trying to make sculpted dolls!)

"Way Opens" Scarf

The Quaker idea of "way opening" usually happens when we are ready for it, when we are open to possibilities. When we listen to our hearts and explore our gifts, we can make connections we never would have expected. We find guides in people, in dreams, in books, in the "still, small voice."

This simple "Way Opens" Scarf is designed as a metaphor for these mystical portals in our lives. It has a surprise "opening" hidden within the back loop double crochet rows. Pulling the long end of the scarf through the opening secures its length warmly around your neck. In the making, you will employ a wonderful and versatile technique for extending a row of stitches without making a separate chain.

INTENTION

To make a "Way Opens" Scarf as a reminder to prepare and watch for the portal of synchronicity, a divine door opening.

MATERIALS

- about 260 yards of worsted weight yarn (I used 2 skeins of Taos from Crystal Palace Yarns.)
- size I or J crochet hook (I used a Susan Bates hook.)
- scissors
- yarn needle

DIRECTIONS

Scarf is worked lengthwise 58 to 60 inches, 5 to 6 inches wide. Chain 203 stitches loosely.

Row 1: Double crochet in the fourth chain from the hook (chain counts as 1 stitch) and in each chain across (200 stitches). Turn.

Row 2: Chain 3 (counts as 1 stitch), skip first stitch, double crochet in the back loop of each stitch across the row, double crochet in the turning chain, turn (200 stitches). This is the right side of the work. You can either mark it with a pin or stitch marker, or simply remember that you are working on the right side when the starting tail is on the right.

Rows 3–5: Work as for row 2 (200 stitches).

Row 6: Chain 3, double crochet in back loop, 124 stitches (125 stitches including the turning chain).

Ready to insert hook into the base of the last stitch.

Work the opening: Yarn over, insert the hook into the base of the last back loop double crochet, draw up a loop, yarn over and pull through to make a chain in that loop, complete the double crochet as usual. One foundation double crochet made. Make 13 more foundation double crochet stitches, first inserting the hook into the chain of the previous stitch, then pulling up a loop, making a chain in it and completing the double crochet.

Rejoin to the row below: Skip 14 stitches of the row below, yarn over and insert the hook into the chain of the fourteenth foundation stitch, draw up a loop, insert the hook into the back loop of the next stitch in the row below, yarn over and pull through, yarn over and pull through 3 loops, yarn over and pull through 2 loops.

Double crochet in back loop in the remaining stitches of the row below. Turn.

Rows 7–10: Work as for row 2. End off. Thread in ends.

FURTHER IDEAS

- Try stepping outside your comfort zone when you choose a color for your scarf. If you are usually drawn to pastels, try a jewel tone or an earth tone. If you often choose primary colors, consider a rich, dark color or a pale, misty one. Branching out is a good beginning to open up creativity.

- Consider working your scarf in stripes. Since the pattern is worked lengthwise, your finished scarf will display long, vertical bands of color.

- Work your scarf in some beautiful, hand-painted yarn for interest.

- Make your scarf up in your favorite solid color and add any embellishments that please you, such as pompoms, tassels, braid, beads, flowers, and the like.

- Give a "Way Opens" scarf as a gift to a friend who is facing an important life decision.

8

From Heart to Hand

Sharing Our Craft

MANY WAYS

The act of sharing is a gesture of giving from one heart to another, from one hand to another. Shared food and drink comfort body and soul. Shared experiences improve understanding. Shared skills, passed from one person to another, enrich everyone and create common ground for work and pleasure.

Guiding someone in learning a new skill is a living testimony to the value of sharing. When my young friend Toddy showed me how to make a square in single crochet, she gave me not only a creative seed I could expand upon but also a practical craft that I could, in turn, share with others. Those are big gifts, wrapped up into the tidy package of one small crochet stitch!

Once we learn to crochet, we all become potential teachers of our craft. We don't need a certificate of education; we need only an interested student and a little patience. Potential students are everywhere—in local schools, churches, nursing homes, community centers, recreational facilities, even next door. There are people of all ages and backgrounds who can benefit from learning to crochet and then gladly pass the skill on to others.

Maybe you've come across the story of three young, surf-loving guys in California who started crocheting beanies "just for fun."

They loved it so much, and their beanies were so popular, that they started thinking about how they might take their hobby to another level. One of them, who had worked for a nonprofit organization in Uganda, proposed, "This might sound crazy, but I think we should teach women in Uganda to crochet." His argument made sense: There weren't many jobs for Ugandan women and, if they learned to crochet, they would have a unique marketable skill. After months of preparation, getting a business plan together, and securing non-profit status for their organization Krochet Kids International (www.krochetkidsinternational.com), a team of twelve landed in Uganda with bags of yarn, hooks, and resilient enthusiasm. Can you imagine the surprise of the local women when these surfers began teaching them to crochet beanies? Yet one beanie at a time, crochet skills are being passed on, making a difference in the lives of untold numbers of women.

Children, too, can benefit from learning handwork skills such as knitting and crochet. They seem to understand instinctively that these are skills with which they can create things for themselves and make special gifts for others. Perhaps most important, when children engage in rhythmic fiber activities, they experience the same calming and renewing effect that adults do. Their fast-paced world is slowed for a time, and their thoughts are given an opportunity to catch up with their busy lives.

I remember reading a story about a high school student who would go to her room and unwind her psyche as she unwound a ball of yarn in the act of crocheting. She would show her mother the length of fabric she had produced and then go back to her room, rip out the work, and wind the yarn back onto the ball, where it would be ready the next time she needed a calming activity. For her, it wasn't about making anything; it was about centering herself and regaining a sense of balance.

While most of us create a specific project as we center ourselves with our crochet, we often have a third purpose in mind: to comfort another person. Even a crocheter who doesn't know anyone in need has access to the many charities that distribute the warmth and love of handmade items. Numbers of small, grassroots organizations with specific target areas have sprung up in the last decade. Some need donated hats, mittens, and scarves for poor families or homeless people; others focus on security blankets or toys for children. Unusual projects include stoma covers for people who have tracheotomies and bandages for leprosy patients (see the Crouse Hospital website at www.crouse.org/news/crochet.html for a free stoma-cover pattern). There are numerous charitable organizations for any crocheter to find a match for her skills and interests, and I have included the stories of eight such organizations later in this chapter.

When we teach our craft and when we make things to comfort others, whether our caring is for family at home or for our brothers and sisters around the globe, the possibilities for community connection are endless. And, as Kristin Spurkland says in her introduction to *Crochet from the Heart*, "Community service makes a difference in the lives of not only the population receiving the service, but in the lives of the givers as well."

SHARING FAITH

Another way that we can share our crochet skills is by expressing our connection to our Creator through the symbols of our faith. Lacy crocheted angels can grace holiday mantels. Threadwork covers can protect and bear witness to the treasured status of sacred texts. Scenes from sacred stories or images of devotion are often designed into the grids of filet crochet. Head coverings are visual symbols of respect and reverence for God in several religious traditions, and many of these are crocheted.

In many places, the most frequently observed crocheted head covering is the Jewish skullcap, called yarmulke in Yiddish and *kippah* in Hebrew. At Temple Beth El in Williamsburg, Virginia, where I live, the very youngest members, both boys and girls, are welcomed into the fold with their own crocheted, baby-sized yarmulke as a symbol of their connection to God and to their faith community.

Crocheted yarmulke by
Ethyl Sternberg.

Ethyl Sternberg crochets these gifts, which she gives to the temple for the rabbi to distribute to new babies and their parents. Sternberg's pint-sized yarmulkes are finely crafted in thin cotton thread. Sternberg starts at the crown and works down the caps, usually working in tones of white or ecru. The caps sometimes sport stripes or outlines of the Star of David in a pastel color. The star designs vary. One might be worked as a solid figure with open spaces around it; another might be crocheted in an openwork technique. Each yarmulke is as different as the diminutive head it will grace.

The newest members of the temple usually wear their yarmulkes for the first time to mark a special occasion. For the girls, that occasion might be their naming ceremony, when they receive their religious name (usually Hebrew or Yiddish in origin). This ritual is called *simchat bat* or *brit bat*. The boys might wear theirs for their *brit* (ceremonial circumcision) or for a later presentation in the temple.

It is clear that the children become emotionally attached to their baby yarmulke. I learned of one boy who keeps his in his "treasure drawer," and Sternberg twinkled with delight as she told me of another, who upon preparing for his Bar Mitzvah, requested that she add rows to his yarmulke so that he could wear it for this important celebration of his growth in the faith.

Sternberg also enjoys crocheting and knitting many other items. When I visited her artful home, she showed me colorful coverlets and boxes with nestled baby things awaiting great-grandchildren. When I asked her what she liked best about crocheting, she told me that it was a feeling of "accomplishment." She certainly has accomplished much and with a sense of purpose.

Sternberg grew up in Germany during a time when everyone learned handwork of all kinds, but she doesn't remember who might have shown her how to loop thread into functional and meaningful items. As she grew into adolescence, Germany developed a dark and destructive side, and the fifteen-year-old and her brother were sent out of the country. Today, eighty-three-year-old Ethyl Sternberg regularly visits high schools and colleges to share her firsthand knowledge of the Holocaust. Her little crocheted yarmulkes are a symbol of something much deeper than simple adherence to religious rules and rituals.

SHARING CROCHET WITH KNITTERS

"I've never seen snow melt and leave pollen behind," Margaret said of our April snow and ensuing burst of spring here in tidewater Virginia.

Three new fiber friends were sitting in my small, spare living room, sharing tea, chocolate chip cookies—and crochet. Although Margaret knew some crochet basics and Valerie had learned some basics as a young child, Helen was as new to knitting as she was to crochet. However, all three women considered themselves knitters, first. But with a nod to the old saying, "If life gives you apples, make applesauce," I took the approach, "If life gives you knitters, teach them how to crochet." (Make sure, of course, that they are amenable to the idea!)

Valerie and I met first. We had both been having a good, long look at the knitting and crochet volumes in one of our local bookstores when we started up a conversation. When Valerie told me that she had learned how to crochet when she was young, she added that she had mostly knitted since then but that she would like to reacquaint herself with crochet. As we talked, we discovered that we had lots of other things in common. We ended up sitting on the carpeted bookstore floor, between shelving, enjoying each other's company so much that we didn't even think to get up for tea and a café seat.

Margaret and Helen were a package deal. Someone at the local coffee shop had told me some women usually crocheted over coffee before going on to their yoga class. It turned out to be a case of mistaken identity—not of people but of the craft. When I made it a point to go to the shop to meet them, I discovered they were actually knitting, not crocheting. But, as with Valerie, the conversation turned from comfortable to downright exciting. Kindred spirits can't be denied!

Now, in my living room, we were all together for the first time. After introductions went around, Margaret showed us two easy-to-make knitted capelets she had completed in thick and thin yarns, one in jewel tones and one in earthy colors. Valerie was wearing a pair of her beautifully cabled red socks with bright gold heels and toes. Helen had brought an eye-catching bag that was crocheted in geometric patterns with yarns that looked hand-dyed. I pulled out my own private trunk show that included beanbags, hats, mittens, baby wear, and yarn dolls dressed in crocheted hats and scarves, along with a couple of felting experiments, a bright color-worked pillow cover, and a blanket. My intent was to show that a large range of techniques are possible with crochet and that crochet can be soft and supple. Everyone was surprised, especially at how malleable the crocheted projects were.

As we settled in, Margaret and Valerie were familiar enough with crochet that they could make their starting chains and work their first row of single crochet, but they both wanted to learn how to do back-loop and front-loop crochet. They were soon on their way, Margaret with a fine, fuzzy pink yarn and Valerie with a patterned sock yarn. I then showed Helen how to make a chain and gave her time to get used to the feel of the hook in her hand.

As is usually the case with those learning to crochet, they preferred the work after the first couple rows were completed. Valerie called the first two rows "a bit fiddly." Not to be deterred, though, she said that she particularly liked the idea of combining knitting and crochet. Margaret agreed that both knitting and crochet set up a nice rhythm and led to creative ideas. Then Helen reminded me of something I have always loved about crochet: she said that holding the work directly in her hands felt intimate and made her hands feel integral to the work.

Crochet doesn't need a frame to hold it rigid as weaving does; it doesn't require needles to keep stitches from unraveling as knitting does. Each stitch falls free as it is completed, becoming an integral part of an ongoing design. There is also an intimate discipline in crochet. We must learn the anatomy of our stitches, learn the various effects of hook placement, and focus our attention so we don't skip a stitch. Intimacy is integral to the craft, and we increase that closeness when we get to know our materials, learn its lessons well, and work with care.

We most often think of intimacy in terms of human relationships, describing our close interactions with another person. Yet I think intimacy also describes our relationship with the arts and crafts that we love. I particularly enjoy playing wind instruments such as recorders and pennywhistles because my fingers cover the holes directly, rather than pressing on keys that, in turn, cover the holes. I delight in crochet because my growing project flows directly into my hands, and I draw a feeling of warmth and nearness.

Warmth and nearness are not casual byproducts, either of crochet or friendships. Integral to deep intimacy is deep respect—respect for unique characteristics, for distinctive beauty, for patient learning. Love is required, along with time and effort. Intimacy is more than a heart connection; true intimacy connects at the physical, mental, and emotional levels. For me, teaching others to crochet is a beautiful way of sharing my intimate connection with my craft.

SHARING CROCHET WITH CHILDREN

Our hands and hearts perform a special task when we share the love of our craft with children. Children need to interact with caring and accepting adults who can teach them new skills. Adults need to connect with the fresh excitement of youth. I can't think of a more energizing way of bringing our contemplative practice into the realm of action than to share our love of handwork with children.

When I was teaching kindergarten, joy, that rare but plainly spiritual commodity, reigned in my classroom by the end of the year. I attribute it to several things, but I believe the most important was finger chains, the foundation of crochet. Late in the first half of the year, I cut strands of thick, soft yarn into six-yard lengths. Then, starting with the older children, I made slip knots for each student and showed him or her how to pull the supply strand through one loop to make another loop. Katie learned first, then Allyson, Connor, and Marissa. As they started, they worked the chains on their laps, soon picking them up and working them adroitly in the air, eventually working so quickly that they used several strands of yarn at one sitting. In this classroom, based on Rudolph Steiner's educational ideas to encourage imagination, the children didn't need to be told what to do with their completed chains. Their chains quickly became crowns, belts, ropes, necklaces, harnesses, and snakes.

One day, we had a visiting child from another Steiner school who also knew how to make finger chains. With this skill in common, he and the other children soon set up shop and became busily engrossed, "manufacturing" and "selling" their finger chains to one another. A few days later, my young entrepreneurs also began to see their glorious creations as gifts. They gave them to parents, sibling's teachers, friends, and me. (One of these gifts still hangs on the door of my wardrobe, where it is very useful for holding hair clips when they are not in use.) By the end of the year, the older children could make their own slip knots and help the younger children when their chains got twisted. Making something useful, sharing knowledge, building skills, and giving gifts all became an integral part of their classroom experience.

They were so proud of those chains! It seemed fitting that they wanted to hang their thick, brightly colored ropes around the edges of the shade tent as we prepared for our springtime celebration— chains in shades of blues and greens, mixed brights and springtime pastels, draped like bunting in loopy scallops around the green tent edges; flags of both pride and joy.

While I observed the children's outward behavior, I was also aware that something much deeper was happening to them. My hyper child ceased to be hyper. My younger children had closed the gap between themselves and the older ones. My older children had become helpers, no longer looking down their noses at the younger ones. They all felt good about themselves. Their ability to focus had grown, and most importantly, they had become a community.

What my children could not have consciously known, and what I came to think about only recently, is that in learning a skill like crochet we experience the unification of two spiritual companions that are often considered separate and unequal: contemplation and action. When we find ways to integrate the disparate parts of ourselves and of our lives, a feeling of wholeness emerges. Activities such as crochet teach us how to live in balance.

As we move from the pole of quiet thoughtfulness to the pole of activity and purpose, we learn what proportion of each we need in our lives. Eventually, we learn to invite bits of one into the other: ideas for action come from contemplation, and ideas to contemplate come from our activities. This is true whether we are talking about the simple act of crocheting with our hands while allowing our minds respite, or talking about the broader patterns of our busy lives.

This active and contemplative dance of crochet took a different form when I taught it to my high school students in First Day School. I gave each student a small bag that contained a hook, a ball of yarn, and a card to identify his or her work. I also supplied two pieces of cardboard cut into seven-by-nine-inch rectangles so they could measure their crocheted pieces as they worked. Then I helped those who only needed a brush-up and taught those who didn't already know how to crochet.

Often we would contemplate the ideas in Kahlil Gibran's *The Prophet* as we kept our hands busy crocheting rectangles that could later be sewn into a blanket. One of my favorite sections of *The*

Prophet that I shared with my students was Almustafa's statement, "It is well to give when asked, but it is better to give unasked through understanding." Then I talked about Jesus's teaching that if a man sues you and asks for your coat, you should also give him your shirt, giving more than is asked. I also told them about something I had heard about giving: you can give as soon as you are in possession of something worth sharing. These three different ideas created a multidimensional picture of giving and provided plenty of food for thought as we worked.

As we read and talked, we added more soft, colorful rectangles to a slowly growing pile that we would send to Warm Up America!, an organization that would sew the pieces together to make a blanket for a person in need. It was the perfect project for us. Even though we couldn't produce enough material for a complete blanket, we could make as many seven-by-nine-inch blocks as we were capable of and know that those pieces would be used well.

My students and I were being contemplatives together, and we were being activists together at the same time. Each activity complemented the other. Crochet is a quiet enough activity to allow for thoughtful conversation, and it is a wonderful vehicle for service. These students experienced the joy of giving of themselves, knowing that they were giving without being asked, giving as much as they were able, and giving as soon as they had the skills to make it possible.

If you would enjoy sharing your crochet skills with young people near you, the best places to start are often those closest to home: young relatives, children in your faith community, students in your own classroom, if you teach, and youth groups such as scouts. If you are especially energetic and have some organizational skills, you might consider teaching in a larger venue, such as an after-school program or a YMCA, or you might offer to start a volunteer handwork program. A helpful resource for teaching larger numbers of children is the Needle Arts Mentoring Program, which was created as a project of the Helping Hands Foundation to link children who are interested in learning needlework skills with caring adults during after-school time slots. You can find out whether there is already an NAMP in your area, or get information on how to start one, at their website, www.needleartsmentoring.org.

Whether you choose to teach only one child, a few, or many, you will be sharing yourself and your skills in invaluable ways and providing for the physical, intellectual, and emotional growth of your student(s). Even beyond these important developmental gifts, you will be sharing the unspoken undercurrents of creativity, common ground, and compassion that will nurture children's souls for a lifetime.

SHARING COMFORT

Compassion is the life-giving and sustaining core at the heart of our humanity, as well as our faith traditions. When we experience compassion, we go beyond intellectual understanding toward a deeper, more sympathetic view of others. We are able to see with the inner eye of tolerance, acceptance, and mutuality. Not only are we are better able to sense the needs of others, but we also feel better about ourselves when our vision of others is clear and deep. The medieval philosopher and theologian Thomas Aquinas went so far as to equate compassion with happiness, saying, "If you want others to be happy, practice compassion. If you want to be happy, practice compassion."

I believe our capacity for compassion, like intelligence, can be developed, guided, and nurtured. Each time we bind heart to hands in our stitches, each time we put contemplation into action, each time we give away our creations of love, we can share comfort and reap satisfaction in our giving. When I self-published my Community Crochet patterns, I included contact information for one or two charitable organizations that would like to receive the finished items. Now, nearly ten years later, as I researched charitable organizations that welcomed crocheted projects, it was like looking in on old friends. Many of the groups I found were ones I had contacted years before about my original patterns. It was such a delight to see their extended websites, long lists of local chapters, letters of thanks, archives of publicity, and plenty of patterns. I invite you to read their stories, pick a project, and join many others in making the world a softer, warmer place for someone in need.

Afghans for Afghans

I was led to Afghans for Afghans through the American Friends Service Committee (AFSC). The AFSC, originally founded in 1917 to help young men receive conscientious objector status and to provide opportunities for alternative service, expanded its mission after World War I to feed and care for refugees, rebuild homes, and aide in agricultural rehabilitation around the globe. Acting in partnership with AFSC, Afghans for Afghans describes their work as "a humanitarian and educational people-to-people project that sends hand-knit and crocheted blankets and sweaters, vests, hats, mittens, and socks to the beleaguered people of Afghanistan."

Ann Rubin, who founded Afghans for Afghans, was moved to do so because of her firsthand experience with Afghan refugees during a visit to Peshawar, Pakistan. When she returned to the United States, she was aided in her cause by AFSC and her local Afghan-American community. When she became aware of a blanket drive being held by these two groups, she immediately thought that handmade blankets should also be created and sent, as symbols of caring from one unknown heart to another.

Afghans for Afghans is an especially good organization for crocheters who love to work with wool. Only wool items and warm items made from animal fibers are accepted because nothing else can truly warm people during the bitterly cold winters in Afghanistan. You can use your own patterns (nothing lacy or open), or you can check out the website (www.afghansforafghans.org). In the section called "Guidelines and Address," you will find measurements for the needed afghans (only complete ones are accepted), notes about color, design, and fiber, as well as a list of printable crochet patterns.

Warming Families

I love the idea behind the Warming Families project. As they say on their website, "the blessings and benefits of helping others go in both directions. Just as families who receive are strengthened, so are families who give.... Families become united in their goal, and children learn by example as selfless giving builds character and returns an immediate sense of accomplishment and personal fulfillment."

This site is loaded with suggestions for ways that families can get involved, starting with some wonderful patterns to crochet and then either distribute locally or through a Warming Families collection site. My favorite patterns are for thick, crocheted socks in sizes to fit men, women, and children, and there is an added template for designing your own socks. You will also find an extra-easy bootee pattern and a very nice baby sweater.

Not everyone in your family has to crochet to participate in the Warming Families project. There are lists of recommended books to help you explain to your children the plight of needy people. There is also a list of other ideas to get your family involved, such as creating "helping bags" (small bags of snacks and toiletries) for shelters. To print out patterns and find more information, including success stories and photos, go to www.warmingfamilies.com.

Care Wear

Bonnie Hagerman founded Care Wear in 1991 when she saw a need to supply preemies with hats and bootees, kimonos, blankets, bibs, and simple toys. Few of us realize how important it is for parents of preemies to have beautiful baby clothes to dress their infants in and how hard it is to find clothing in preemie sizes. Bonnie has also received many requests for items sized to fit healthy, full-term babies, and she suggests that most hospitals welcome extra blankets (about thirty-by-thirty inches). It is sad, but another big need is for something beautiful in which to dress the premature babies who don't survive their struggle for life.

Bonnie has a nice list of crochet patterns on her website, www. carewear.org, including many adorable preemie-sized hats, tiny mittens, and booties. Some of the little hats are seasonal, and some are whimsical. You will also find the instructions for a very pretty burial gown or a one-piece burial suit.

Visit the section on Bonnie's website called "Join" (which simply means to help!) to find out the best place for you to donate and what might be most needed. She also provides a lot of helpful advice about contacting local hospitals.

Project Linus

Project Linus is the contribution of Karen Loucks, who was moved by a story in *Parade* magazine about a very sick child and her security blanket. As a knitter, Karen recognized how comforting a handmade "blankie" could be. It is natural, then, that her organization's mission statement begins, "It is our mission to provide love, a sense of security, warmth and comfort to children who are seriously ill, traumatized or otherwise in need through the gifts of new, handmade blankets and afghans, lovingly created by volunteer 'blanketeers.'"

As Karen started to put her ideas into action, she not only knitted blankets for children in need, but also shared her thoughts with and collected blankets from others. Eventually, she asked Peanuts cartoon creator Charles Schultz for permission to name her project after his character Linus, who is never without his security blanket.

Project Linus has grown substantially since it was founded in 1995, and Karen has passed on its operational duties to other capable hands. She has returned her attention to her job as an emergency medical technician in a children's hospital, where she has the privilege of handing out blankets herself.

If you are interested in being a "blanketeer," you can find information about a chapter near you, get help, and find patterns at www.projectlinus.org. If you want to use your own blanket patterns, please keep in mind that many of the donated blankets will go to hospitals and that medical technicians prefer blankets with more closed stitch patterns to prevent them from getting hung up on equipment.

Head Huggers

Head Huggers is an organization that distributes warm, soft caps for people who have lost their hair. You may be aware of the phrase "chemo caps," which is used to describe special hats for people who have lost hair due to chemotherapy, but there are many other reasons for hair loss, such as brain surgery, burns, and alopecia areata (an autoimmune disease that causes hair to fall out).

Sue Thompson, the founder of Head Huggers, is a physician who was still making the occasional house call before she retired in 1997. She started making warm caps after she had lunch with a woman who was going through chemotherapy and who wore a baseball cap to keep her head warm. Lamenting that it was a shame that this woman had to endure a cold head on top of cancer and all that it entailed, Sue went home and made her a few soft caps. The thought began to take hold in her mind that there were probably a lot of people similarly in need of soft head coverings.

As Sue passed the word around about the need for these caps and collected patterns, as donated caps started coming in and organizations put in requests for them, Head Huggers took on a visible form. Although Sue felt overwhelmed occasionally, she believed that there was a higher power at work as friends, relatives, and acquaintances lent their various talents to her vision. There are now fifty-two satellite Head Huggers groups that have distributed over 35,000 caps all over the country.

In a letter Sue sent me about the history of Head Huggers, she told a funny story about one of the mannequins she uses to model her hat samples. She had purchased a scratched and dented mannequin on an Internet auction site, and her nephew had been able to remove the marks with a photo touch-up device so she could use the mannequin to "model" the hats on the Head Huggers website. However, after repeated attempts to make her mannequin look better, Sue gave up and took her to a Merle Norman cosmetics studio. The mannequin got a free makeover.

If you go to www.headhuggers.org and click on "See all the hat patterns," you will find photos and patterns for a variety of crocheted caps to warm the heads of both adults and children. (And you might catch more than one glimpse of the made-over mannequin model.)

Mother Bear Project

If you are a child at heart, the Mother Bear Project website (www.motherbearproject.org) is a fun place to go. On the "Photo Gallery" pages, you can see the joy on the faces of the children who have received their bears and experienced the creativity of many people who have knitted or crocheted colorful variations into the bears' sweaters and pants even though all the bears are made from the same patterns. When you make a bear and send it to Mother Bear Project to distribute, they will add a red felt heart to the bear before it is sent to a child in an emerging country.

Though the bears are fun, Mother Bear Project's mission is a serious one. Most of the bears are presently going to Africa where many sick, needy, and orphaned children are thrilled to have a cuddly friend made by a caring person. Putting their mission statement into action, Mother Bear Project provides "comfort and hope to children, primarily those affected by HIV/AIDS in emerging nations, by giving them a gift of love in the form of hand knit and crocheted bears."

You can order either a knit or crochet version of the instructions on the website. There is a small fee for the versatile and reusable pattern, and Mother Bear Project also requests that you send a small, specified donation along with your bear to help them with packaging and international shipping. You can view photos, updates, and a list of distribution locations on the website. If you don't have time to make a bear yourself, you might consider sponsoring a bear or giving the sponsorship of a bear as a gift.

Snuggles Project

If you have a special place in your heart for animals, the Snuggles Project is a great way to get involved. Initially presented by the organization Hugs for Homeless Animals (www.h4ha.org), the Snuggles Project has grown so much that it now has its own website at www.snugglesproject.org.

President and founder Rae French started the Snuggles Project in 1996 in an effort to comfort animals living in the austere conditions of animal shelters. "Snuggles" are simply security blankets for animals, and they comfort dogs and cats not only physically but also psychologically. It has been observed that animals with snuggles are more likely to be adopted from shelters!

When you visit the Snuggles Project website, you will find a number of patterns for crocheted snuggles, including the Quick and Easy Crocheted Snuggle and the Round Crocheted Snuggle. When you are ready to donate, read the section called "Making a Snuggles Donation" to find out if there is a participating shelter in your area and what you can do if your local shelter is not participating. Then print out your donation form, which the Snuggles Project requests that you include with your donated snuggle. For further information, you can peruse the blog, member forum, and newsletters, which are all available on the website.

Snuggles are great projects for kids and beginners because smaller squares can be sewn together (very securely please) to make a snuggle. Also, the creatures who receive a snuggle aren't going to fuss over small mistakes; they will just be glad for padding and warmth. Since snuggles don't require fine work, people with failing or partial eyesight can often accomplish this worthwhile task.

Warm Up America!

Warm Up America! is probably the best-known yarn-based charity in the country, thanks to Evie Rosen, who started it out of her knitting shop in 1991. Two brilliantly simple ideas are bundled up in her call for seven-by-nine-inch knitted or crocheted sections with which to make afghans. Evie understood the challenge involved in making an entire afghan, so she made it possible for individuals and even the smallest communities to contribute any number of sections and send them to another location to be sewn together. No one person has to make all the sections, and no one person has to do all the construction. The other stroke of genius was to ask for rectangular sections, not square. This makes an afghan automatically proportioned to warm someone in an economical way.

When Evie retired, her national grassroots program was turned over to the Craft Yarn Council of America, where it is now incorporated as a tax-exempt charitable organization. If Evie's unique approach piques your interest, you can start to learn more by visiting the foundation's website at www.warmupamerica.org for an introduction to the organization. Then you can crochet seven-by-nine-inch pieces alone or with friends. If you and your friends have enough to make a forty-nine-piece afghan, you can put it together and donate it to a local shelter, hospital, nursing home, or homeless person. If you don't have the time or energy to complete a whole afghan and distribute it locally, just send those rectangles to Warm Up America!, where your sections will be added to the contributions of others, bound into a usable blanket, and distributed.

You can learn more about Warm Up America! on their website, including where to send your sections. There are also ideas for starting a group, working with children, joining sections, and donating locally.

SHARING BECOMES HEALING

As I started to write this book, I remembered my friend Gail who is a crocheter. We live in distant states and hadn't been in touch for a couple of years. When I called her to ask if she had any crochet stories she might like to share, I was touched by what she told me:

In the winter of 2005, I found myself in a state of depression I hadn't known before. In the previous years, I had noticed a pattern developing that used to be called "winter doldrums," but has more recently been named Seasonal Affective Disorder, but this winter was worse than any before. My doctor recommended a mild anti-depressant, which I took somewhat reluctantly. It helped me function but did nothing for the real problem.

That same winter, a young pregnant woman came to see me, asking my help in placing the baby for adoption. Together, we read through profiles of couples wanting to adopt and selected one couple to meet with. My friend asked me to go with her for moral support when she met them, and as I got to know the couple and thought of the gift this child would be to them, I wanted to do something tangible for them. I hadn't crocheted in some time, but now it seemed the most natural thing to do, to make a baby blanket. I selected a pattern from a book of patterns that featured the Care Bear characters. I chose the bear called the "Wish Bear," because this couple had wished for a child and they were going to receive it.

There were only a couple of months left until the baby was due, so I started the work on the blanket. As I spent time crocheting and thinking about and praying for my friend, the child, and the family that was going to begin, I found my own depression crumbling away. The act of doing something for someone else took my thoughts off myself and opened me up to serving others.

After finishing the blanket for this special little baby, I made another and another—eight so far, each a different pattern. I decided to ask the local women's shelter, if I made more, would they give them to homeless children.

I have never considered myself a creative person. I am an accountant by trade, which is the dictionary opposite of artistic. But crocheting allows me to express some part of myself that otherwise gets lost. It is also an opportunity for me to put into practice the biblical teachings of caring for others.

Sharing crochet, teaching our craft, and giving the fruits of our labor are satisfying, joyful ways of celebrating our work. Helping to keep people and animals warm and comforted by giving bears or hats or snuggles are compassionate ways of putting our contemplation into action. But the act of doing something for someone else can also have a healing effect on us, one fiber, one stitch at a time. Perhaps even more important than the products we create, the process of crocheting can become a spiritual practice of healing for our worn or torn spirits that need mending. As we bring stitches and fabrics together, we create something whole and beautiful out of many disjointed pieces. I can think of no better image, and method, for the healing of our souls.

FROM HEART TO HAND QUERIES

Have you considered sharing your crochet skills with someone else? What that experience was like for you?

Children often do things for the process alone, but sometimes we adults also need this focus. Think of a time when the process of doing something was more important to you than the product. What made that experience different? What about spiritual process?

Have you intentionally sought out other crocheters to share with? How was your experience different from other gatherings with friends?

What project could you make, or teach others to make, that would provide common ground? (Playful projects such as beanbags and yarn dolls with crocheted scarves are good considerations because they can be appreciated across generations.)

How can you get involved in using your handwork skills to care for those in need? Consider what the need might be for warm, hand-made items in your community. You might consider hosting a brain-storming session with like-minded friends to make a list of ideas.

Think of a time when you had a healing experience connected to your crochet work. What was that experience like for you?

Friends and Tea Cozy

We need to celebrate each other and our crochet work more often. Tea parties are a great way to do that. They can be informal, they don't require dues or business meetings, and you can vary the number of friends you invite. You can even hold a tea celebration all by yourself, if that is what fits into your schedule. Crochet and sip!

This tea cozy is worked in an easy side-to-side cable stitch pattern made up of single crochets. The cables are open, making it easy to thread a ribbon through the top after the two parts are sewn together. Your cozy will fit around a four-cup potbelly-style teapot nicely. For a wider cozy, add an extra repeat of the pattern for each of the two pieces. I have included the chain stitch count for the pattern as well, so you can make your tea cozy taller or shorter.

If you are in the middle of a summer heat wave as you read this, remember that a tea cozy can also insulate iced tea. Time to relax!

INTENTION

To remind you to take time out to share a cup of tea, some conversation, your spiritual gleanings, your crochet skills, and your compassion.

MATERIALS

- 1 skein of worsted weight yarn (about 190 yards) (I used Brown Sheep Lamb's Pride.)
- size H or I hook (I used a Susan Bates hook.)
- yarn needle
- scissors
- a yard of ribbon

DIRECTIONS

Gauge: 7 stitches equals 2 inches, 1 four-row repeat equals 1 inch.
This pattern stitch requires a multiple of 3 chains plus 4 extra.

The turning chain does not count as a stitch. Leaving a 12-inch tail, chain 34.

Base Row: Skip 2 chains and work 1 single crochet into third chain from hook, 1 single crochet into each chain across, turn (32 stitches).

Note: Skip row 1 for now and work rows 2 through 4. You will come back to row 1 when the pattern repeats.

Row 1 (wrong side): Chain 1, single crochet in each stitch across, turn (32 stitches).

Note: When working on the backs of the 3 chains on row 2, it is easiest to work into the front loop, which will be uppermost. Remember to always turn your work clockwise so the supply thread is out of the way.

Row 2 (right side): Chain 1, 1 single crochet into the first single crochet of the row below, *chain 3, skip next 2 stitches, 1 single crochet into next stitch, turn to wrong side, 1 single crochet into each of the 3 chains just worked, turn to right side, pull the 3 single crochets forward and work 1 single crochet into each of the 2 skipped stitches, repeat from asterisk to last stitch, 1 single crochet into last stitch, turn (32 stitches). Row 2 is the right side of the work. You will recognize it by your pretty row of cables.

Note: The stitches you work into the wrong side of the cable row will look the same as the two stitches after the first single crochet of the row. Don't worry if you don't insert the hook into exactly the right place. This pattern is forgiving.

Row 3 (wrong side): Chain 1, single crochet into the first stitch of the row below, *2 single crochet into next stitch behind cable, 1 single crochet into next stitch with single crochet in it, skip over single crochet, repeat from asterisk to last stitch, 1 single crochet into last stitch, *turn* (32 stitches).

Right side, 3 chains and single crochet into row below.

Wrong side, single crochet into chains just worked.

Right side, 3 single crochets pulled forward to work single crochet into skipped stitches.

Row 4 (right side): Chain 1, single crochet in each stitch across, turn (32 stitches).

Repeat rows 1 through 4 until there are 7 complete cable repeats. End off leaving a 12-inch tail. Make a second piece.

Finishing: Align the two pieces side by side with the cable rows running vertically and the more open ends of the cables facing down.

Sewing the first seam (this is the seam that goes around the spout). With the right sides facing up, thread the tail at the bottom into a yarn needle and overcast stitch the 2 pieces together for about 2 inches.

Take an extra stitch to help secure the seam, thread in the end and trim. Starting with the tail at the top, sew down 4 inches.

Sewing the second seam: Bring the remaining two edges together side by side with the cables on the outside. Overcast a 4-inch seam from the top down.

Securely sew a ⅞-inch button to one unstitched bottom edge. Make a loop of 10 chains at the other bottom edge. Thread the remaining end into your yarn needle and secure it with several stitches, then thread in the end.

Thread about 30 inches of matching or contrasting ribbon under the cables and 2 or 3 rows down from the top. Pull the ends up, make a bow and trim the ends.

FURTHER IDEAS

- Make a tea cozy as a special gift for someone who is ill or is experiencing a time of grief. This cozy would be a tangible way of sharing comfort.

- Have a tea-cozy-making party to remind friends that every crochet gathering can be celebratory. Teach this pattern to anyone who wants to learn, make a pattern collection, or have a creativity experience.

- Worked in one piece and adjusted to fit, this pattern can be used to make a very cute hat for you or for someone in need. Adjust by making a longer or shorter chain (multiples given at the start of the pattern), working more or fewer rows, and changing the placement of the ribbon.

9

The Creative Spirit

Making Crochet Uniquely Ours

A GENTLE BREEZE

A Friends meeting I attended used to gather in a modern Episcopal church on Sunday afternoons. Since we were a small group, we sat in a circle at the back of the sanctuary. Whenever we looked up, we could see through large windows onto a little woody glade, which was often inhabited by rabbits and birds. At that time of day, the rest of the sanctuary was in shadow, yet there was one object that continually caught my eye and held my attention.

Near the altar hung a simple red felt banner, with a white felt dove. In my imagination, I would make it into a quilted flag with detailed stitching to delineate the feathers, or a painting with the eyes of a resting dove expressing the wisdom of all creatures, or a collage with real feathers attached and a woody branch in its talons.

But what was deeply important to me about this banner was not so much the image but the words on it: *Creator Spiritus*. Not having studied Latin, I didn't know the exact meaning of the phrase, so I was free to play with all the ideas that these two words brought to mind.

It seemed obvious that *Creator* was a way of expressing the idea of God. Quakers believe that there is "that seed of God" in every person, and it warmed my heart to think of my creative life as a miniature version of a divine and universal creativity. The word

Spiritus spoke to me of the wind ruffling every leaf of a plentiful tree at the same time, of breezes that can be felt in the miniscule muscles that encircle the finest hairs on our bodies, of a zephyr that can wind itself around trees and buildings and blow into every crack, through every fiber.

Many inferences came to my mind as I contemplated the juxtaposition of these two words: that the Creator is Spirit, that the Spirit is creative, that creativity is spiritual, that true spirituality is creative. And I wondered how the divine spirit of creativity wafted into the world and made its way into human souls.

Though I didn't have answers to all my questions, one thing I did know about creativity was that it is experiential. It is a firsthand experience, the direct action of my own knowledge, choices, and thoughts on something (usually) material in my world. I am not being creative when I watch television; I am partaking of someone else's creativity. The same is true of listening to music: I can enjoy someone else's creativity, but it is not mine. I have acted as a consumer and not a creator. When we consume, we look outside ourselves for what we think we want and need. Matthew Fox, in his book *Creativity: Where the Divine and the Human Meet*, even proposed that "most addictions come from our surrendering our own real powers, that is, our powers of creativity."

This is not an argument against partaking in another's creativity, but rather a suggestion for a new awareness, a more soul-satisfying balance. As we learn to be creative, we learn to look inward. We learn more about ourselves: Are we patient or agitated when we come to a snag in our work? Are we accepting of the creative works we give birth to or are we judgmental?

As we deepen into our creativity and craft, we may find something else happening: we learn how to best handle our tools, and we develop sensitivity to the materials we are working with. They teach us the lessons of skill if we listen to them, and we discover our unique way with them. For different crocheters, hooks of the same size and shape may produce different effects. Different yarns work best for different projects—and different wearers. Bulky yarn, for instance, might make a warm garment, but will flatter only a few wearers! In listening to ourselves, our tools, and our materials, we develop a special inner ear.

Sometimes we start out with one idea in mind only to have the work take on a life of its own. An idea or a solution will appear out of seeming nothingness. "That wasn't my idea; I was just listening and ready!"

Just as crochet is an intimate craft, so, too, is creativity a form of intimacy—intimacy with our intellect, intimacy with our feelings, a willingness to welcome unseen forces into our lives and enjoy their presence. Matthew Fox wrote that "to speak of creativity is to speak of profound intimacy. It is also to speak of our connecting to the Divine in us and of our bringing the Divine back to community."

As crocheters, I believe we are doing just that.

LAYERS OF CREATIVITY

A year or two after my young friend Toddy first showed me how to make a single-crocheted square, I found instructions for a chain mesh shawl and some granny squares. I set to work on both. I developed a better eye for hook placement, learned more basic stitches, and made some warm things for myself. But, mostly, I was stitching up contentment. A few months later, I found a copy of Susan Morrow and Mark Dittrick's *Contemporary Crochet* at the local bookstore. I read everything they had to say about crochet, and I began to add texture and shaping to my repertoire. I started to play.

I had a large skein of light green yarn, and I wanted to know if, by making treble stitches first, then rows of gradually shorter stitches, I could get the effect of looking into the distance at grass. So I tried it. Hmm ... I had small amounts of several rainbow-colored yarns, so I set about trying to make half circles of color above my grass. Soon I had figured out how to connect sky to the grass and the rainbow. I was charmed. I made a row of blue trebles at the top of my sky, ran a small dowel through them, and hung my rainbow on the wall. I had made it myself!

Hildegard of Bingen once wrote, "God gave to human kind the talent to create with all the world." When we pick out a ball of yarn, whether at the store or from our own stash, then choose a hook (I like to choose hooks in colors that match my yarn or contrast with it), and start stitching, we are creating "with all the world." There is creativity in our choices, in combinations of choice, in colors, textures, and patterns. It is a birthing process. When we make something, we bring something into the world that was not there before. It cannot be just exactly like another person's work no matter how hard we try. It is uniquely ours.

Crochet creativity grows richer by layers, something like the process of building a beautiful cake by layering cake, frosting, cake, pudding, cake, and more frosting. If we use a pattern for a project and tweak it—say, by using a different yarn or pattern stitch, or changing the shape a bit—we are exercising our creativity. If several people in a crochet community use a design idea as a platform for individual creativity, while adhering to a recognizable form, the results can take another creative turn. This often happens in folk art and craft, and the myriad designs of granny squares and ripple patterns are abundant testimony to "variations on a theme" in crochet. No one person owns the basic idea, and almost everyone likes to play with it.

When we start from scratch and make our own design, we add another layer of creativity. We choose the size, shape, construction techniques, stitch pattern, yarn, hook, finishing details, and embellishments to fabricate something unique. At this point, we can claim our work as "original."

We add yet another layer when we set our minds to the task of learning about color, fiber, and design. While creativity turns on the burners of intuition, learning about it lights the whole range. Even those for whom using artistic elements comes as second nature can benefit from some formal study of the subject, whether it is in the form of reading or taking a class. If you take a color class, for example, you might learn more about which yarn colors contrast and which colors blend or dominate. What emotional responses do particular colors elicit?

Color, form, and texture are among the most important design elements of creative crocheting. The form of a project needs to compliment your chosen colors and textures. Purses may be boxy or curvy; a garment, close fitting or loose, fashionable, practical, or both. Do you want a square neckline or a V-neck? Do you desire a softly draped form or one that is thick and warm?

How much texture do you want? You could create a soft, shallow texture by making your project in a basic stitch pattern or one that mixes the basic stitches: single crochet, half double crochet, and double crochet. The simplest example of mixing stitches would be alternating rows of two or three basic stitches. Simple openwork patterns, such as those made with the V-stitch and cluster patterns, offer a more sophisticated look while keeping the texture low. Textured stitches of medium height are often formed of raised stitches and picots. Many crocheters love the craft for the densest of textures possible: bobbles, popcorns, chains, and thick, furry loops.

My favorite design factor is called the "point of interest." The easiest and most fun places to play with points of interest are on the crowns of hats, by adding doodads, such as braids, ropes, tassels, and pompoms.

The way you shape or seam the crown can also be a part of the "interest." Purchased embellishments such as ribbons, buttons, beads, and charms can act as points of interest and add special touches to almost any project. Well-chosen borders and edgings, and the techniques you use to make them, can make an item unique and appealing. But the

Hat with crocheted button at crown, hat with scattered rug knots, mittens with simple cuffs and pompoms.

interest you provide doesn't need to be profuse. A great color pattern or stitch pattern may be all that is needed. Paying attention and making a crocheted item interesting without making it "busy" takes thought and receptivity. You need to sense when to stop as well as when to add. This kind of listening to your projects allows the Divine into your creations.

Even if the layers of your project are all in place, no piece is complete without love. Love is the spiritual element that makes our creations shine. When we care about what we are doing, when we create from a calm center, grounded in the present moment, there is health and balance in our work that brings our projects to life.

I like to think of *art* as a short word nestled inside the word *heart*. When we choose the "right" hook—the one that fits our hand, slips smoothly through our yarn, and makes a beautiful fabric—we are stitching heart into our fabric. When we use a yarn that feels good to the touch, delights us with its color, and looks good in our stitch pattern, "art" and "heart" are both more evident. When we choose materials that are a joy to work with, the work gives back measure for measure.

CROCHET IN COMMUNITY

In the world of folk art, it sometimes happens that a whole community comes to love a needlework design so deeply that they become known for that work. Knitted examples are common, such as cabled Aran patterns, Faire Isle color stranding, a variety of Scandinavian patterns, and the bright stylized images of native animals on South American earlap hats. Finding examples of crocheted folk designs takes us a little farther afield.

Tapestry Crochet

When Carol Norton Ventura lived in South America as a Peace Corps volunteer in the late seventies, she became aware of the tightly worked and densely patterned bags that are made and used by the men in Guatemala. Since her job involved working with a weaving cooperative, she maintained her focus on weaving, only purchasing several of the bags to bring home with her. Once home, her interest in her bright acquisitions piqued, and she unraveled part of a bag to discover its construction secrets. Over the years, Ventura has become a spokesperson for this technique, which she calls "tapestry crochet."

The same spirited color combinations and rhythmic motifs that are found in many other south-of-the-border crafts dance around these Guatemalan bags. Shades of red, purple, pink, and orange are hooked without inhibition, and the bags of each region bear a distinct combination of images. They are worked in single crochet in continuous rounds, and every stitch is made in both loops of the stitch in the row below. Geometric designs and simple representations of local animals and familiar items are worked in color by carrying several strands at a time, catching and covering the colors not in use, inside the stitch being made. This produces a smooth, strong fabric with no loose threads.

Ventura has written several books, including *Tapestry Crochet, More Tapestry Crochet,* and *Beaded and Felted Tapestry Crochet,* and has written numerous articles for magazines. You can find more information about Carol Norton Ventura, the colorful bags from Guatemala, and how to use tapestry crochet techniques to make a variety of projects at www.tapestrycrochet.com.

Korsnas Sweaters

While tapestry crocheted items have found their way into commercial venues outside of South America, there is a Finnish sweater tradition that is rarely seen. I first learned of it from the January/ February 2004 issue of *Piecework* magazine. Because the sweaters from Korsnas have both crocheted and knitted sections, these sweaters were first documented in America in a book entitled *Nordic Knitting* by Susanne Pagold.

Korsnas sweaters are usually pullovers with bright (often red) crocheted yokes, shoulders, cuffs, and hems. The midsections of the bodies and the sleeves usually consist of a knitted seed pattern on a cream ground. Knitted two-stranded color work that blends with the yoke is then worked from the armholes up to where the crocheted yoke starts. The crochet sections are patterned with at least three accent colors, usually on a red ground. Since Korsnas has cultural ties to Sweden, the choice of ground colors and the shapes of the color-worked motifs are Swedish inspired.

The crocheted sections are all worked in back loop single crochet, always from right to left without turning. The front and back pieces may be worked either in the round to the armholes or as flat pieces. The sleeves are worked in continuous rounds from the top down, decreasing as needed. The sleeve shoulders and cuffs are created in a similar fashion to the Guatemalan bags, and they are firm from the unused colors being carried inside the stitches.

"Many of the Korsnas sweaters in the museum collections, although worn for many years, are in remarkably good condition," Carol Huebscher Rhoades, the author of the article in *Piecework*, observed. "The crocheted sections, particularly those at the neck and lower edges, kept the garment from stretching out with wear; worn-out cuffs and other edges could be replaced. The well-spun yarns, multistrand patterning and excellent workmanship made the sweaters durable and warm, but heavy: a Korsnas sweater can easily weigh 2 pounds."

Oyas

I had always assumed that sturdiness and usefulness must be a factor in a people's love of their crocheted or knitted art, that beauty combined with practicality was a large part of the craft. Then I discovered a little-known folk craft called *oyasi*. This Turkish lace seemed, at first, to exist for beauty alone. *Oyas* are like tiny garlands worked onto sashes, headscarves, handkerchiefs, towels, and fabrics used to wrap and store items of clothing. Though *oyas* can be created using a variety of techniques, my favorite type is called *tig oyasi* and is crocheted in very fine threads to represent flowers, fruits, and leaves. Ann Stearns, author of *The Batsford Book of Crochet*, describes *tig oyasi* as "direct replicas in miniature of Turkish wild flowers such as violets, orchids, pansies, roses, jasmines, carnations, strawberries, blackberries, mulberries and peppers."

Needlework in Turkey is still handed down from mother to daughter, friend to friend, without written instruction. Because designs were passed from region to region and modified, over time, certain patterns are now found in particular regions.

The earliest and best-quality *oyas* are needlemade, using techniques that may date back as far as the eighth century BCE. When crochet hooks became available, women quickly realized that it was easier to work with a continuous strand than to constantly rethread a needle. *Oyas* can also be tatted or worked in hairpin lace, and all these techniques may incorporate beads. In Turkey, rich and poor women alike made these beautiful laces, and a few still do. Those less well off made theirs in a cottage industry while more well-to-do women gave theirs as gifts.

It turns out that *oyasi* do have a purpose beyond beauty. In traditional Turkish culture, women were not allowed to speak to their mothers-in-law until they had their first child or until two years had passed. They could signal how they were feeling, how they felt about their husbands, even how they felt about their mothers-in-law, by the symbolism in their *oyas*.

How does a country's folk craft come to be revered? If a craft is to survive in its own culture and then be enjoyed by others, love of the craft must come first. In each of these examples, the designs and motifs also express the people's love of the natural world and their cultural symbols. Their work identifies them visually with their family, community, or region. Probably even more important, the one-on-one teaching of the craft enforces familial bonds. Yet even if a craft flourishes in geographical pockets indefinitely, if the finished works never cross borders, the craft will not spread. Cultural crafts become known only if travelers take photographs, describe them in writing, or purchase a few of the items to bring home to their own towns and villages.

As was the historical case with Irish crochet, when both a voracious appetite for inexpensive lace and a desperate need to make money with little overhead combined to spread the craft, items such as the Guatemalan bags feed our appetite for color and have become sought after. Thanks to Carol Norton Ventura, the skill will be passed on in writing. Although neither the Korsnas sweaters nor the Turkish *oyas* currently have a broad market, that, too, could change. But for now, both continue out of a love of a people for their particular craft.

You might ask, "What is so important about folk crochet?" I propose that folk crafts welcome us into a form of timelessness. They are another way to understand the concept of what it means to "be in the moment." The poet Rumi expressed this idea in two lines: "Come out of the circle of time, / And into the circle of love."

Folk crafts take us "out of the circle of time": they are neither old nor young, neither trendy nor out of date. Transcending time brings us "into the circle of love": we are enfolded into the community of those who have gone before us, those who are with us now, and those who will come after us.

Each new variation becomes our creative mark on the world and enables us to take our place among other creators in an expression of divine creativity. Our collective creativity becomes a unity that forms a timeless wholeness.

PRACTICING CREATIVITY WITH CROCHET

Creativity can be shy. How many times have you felt vulnerable when you started to create something on your own? Criticism can worm its way into our minds and, once settled (especially if it began at an early age), can continue to sabotage us by repeating itself every time we try to initiate a creative activity. To take creative action, we need to have a sense that we are capable of doing what we want to do and what we set out to do.

One way to quell the negative voices and replace them with a nurturing chorus is to practice some form of meditation even before you pick up your crochet hook. This will help you stay in touch with your true center so you can exercise your will over the ill will of the creativity censor. Or you might try leveling criticism with affirmation. In her book *The Artist's Way*, Julia Cameron offers fifteen affirmations, such as "I now treat myself and my creativity more generously" and "My creativity blesses others." You might enjoy creating your own similar affirmations or collecting them from other sources. My personal favorite is a quote from Goethe: "Whatever you think you can do or believe you can do, begin it, for action has magic, grace, and power in it."

The key word in Goethe's quote is *action*. Action suggests starting right where you are, affirming your creativity, and getting out your crochet. If you take just one step at a time, you will reach your destination.

Do you know the basic crochet stitches? Do you know some shaping techniques? Maybe your next step is to try a pattern that incorporates several stitches at once so that you get used to switching from one stitch to another.

Can you read patterns? Start with a very simple project that is written in abbreviations. Think of abbreviations and diagrams as simple puzzles and try them just for fun. Don't worry about product. Just enjoy the puzzling out that is part of the process.

Maybe you know the basics and have started to shape original gifts from them. Try making swatches of stitch patterns that are new to you. After you complete each swatch, brainstorm what you might like to use that stitch pattern for. Write your ideas down on an index card. Think of that stitch pattern worked in a heavier yarn or a very fine one. Imagine it in different colors. Would it shape easily into a triangular shawl or a simple sweater? Would it make a dressy mitten, scarf, and hat set, or a sturdy child's jacket? After you have let your creative imagination have its say, tie the index card to the swatch. You might even enjoy covering a shoe box with pretty paper and using it only to keep your swatches.

You might want to purchase a stitch pattern book that will enlarge your understanding of the rich possibilities that crochet has to offer. One of my favorites is *Harmony Guide to Crocheting* by Debra Mountford. But beware: you may not be able to stop at just one book!

When we are caught up in creativity, for a short time we can behold the world as if it were new to us, as if we had just made our first block tower or discovered that three pebbles can be laid out in a line or a triangle. Creativity is like nature; it is playful and it is plentiful. Let it flow. As Julia Cameron so beautifully puts it, "Our creativity is our gift from God. Our use of it is our gift to God. Accepting this bargain is the beginning of true self-acceptance."

THE CREATIVE SPIRIT QUERIES

What are the differences between the way you think about your creative activity inwardly versus outwardly? For example, have you felt inwardly that your creativity is a spiritual endeavor, but felt outwardly as though the creative activities you love are frivolous?

When you are involved in creative projects, do you feel more centered? How does this affect other aspects of your life?

What new insights have you gained about yourself through your craft? How do the acts of carving out time and space for your craft, gathering your tools and materials, and adding to your skills at a comfortable pace make you feel about your approach to other parts of your life?

Have you ever been aware of creative ideas or solutions to problems coming to you as though they came from "somewhere else"?

How might your crochet experiences be different if you learned how to work your projects from another person rather than from a book?

Do you have a naysayer in your head? What practices do you use to quiet this influence?

Creativity isn't only about the things we make, but also about how we approach our relationships, our living spaces, and our lives. In what ways, other than crochet, do you exercise your creativity?

Scrumbled Tea Steeper

Scrumbling, a kind of free-form crochet, is the most experiential and intimate method of crocheting I know. It calls on us to use our creativity and our intuition. It allows Spirit into our work and invites us to play and listen at the same time. And we create a small work of art, just large enough to cover a cup of steeping tea, a sleepy child's morning cocoa, or a distracted husband's coffee.

INTENTION

To make a beverage cover that will free your creativity and then contain the warmth of your brew.

MATERIALS

- whatever hooks and yarns "call" to you
- a piece of wool felt slightly smaller than your finished piece (alternatively, a piece of fabric; iron-on interfacing optional)
- any decorative materials you choose

DIRECTIONS

No Rules

There are no rules! Here are some possibilities to get you started:

- Chain any number of stitches.

- Start as to work in a circle or as though you are starting a square, or a triangle, or an oval.

- Turn whenever you wish and work in a new direction.

- Change colors whenever you wish.

• End off and start again in a different place.

• Use any number of colors.

• Make textured stitches such as bobbles, popcorns, and picots, or leave the surface flat.

• Work some stitches in the back loops and then later add stitches into the front loops, which remain free.

No Rules?

Well, there are just a *few* rules for this project, even though scrumbling itself isn't bound to traditional crochet rules.

Since you'll want your tea steeper to sit flat on top of your cup, the main part should be flat. However, if you like, you can work sides for it that will increase its insulating qualities.

Your finished piece should be large enough to cover the mug you want to use it on.

Your steeper needs to be firm enough so that it won't collapse into your drink. I used a G hook and worsted weight yarns to make a more firm fabric. I also used a lot of single crochets to add body. And I used half double crochets and double crochets judiciously until I got to the outer edge.

Working Notes

While you make your tea steeper, you will probably be collecting many yarn ends on the underside of the work. Don't worry. You will be sewing a simple piece over the bottom, so you can tie pairs of ends together and trim them leaving an inch or so of yarn. You can thread in with a yarn needle ends that need redirecting or extra tucking. Also thread in the ends on the outer edges where they might show.

As you work, you may find that you don't like an addition you have made. Don't be afraid to pull out stitches that you don't like. If you come to dislike something in the middle of your piece, try working another group of stitches over it. I made a ruffled segment in a yarn that was too dark as I worked on my first steeper. It stood up from the rest of the work so I just cut across it and pulled out the loose ends. Scrumbling can be a good lesson in transforming negatives into positives and coming to accept the way that creativity moves through us even if it is not exactly what we had planned.

Finishing Up

Thread in the ends at the edge of your work. Knot and trim interior ends. Cut a piece of good quality wool felt slightly smaller than your steeper and sew it to the bottom, covering your knots and yarn ends. (It is a good idea to pin it down to keep it from sliding while you work.) As an alternative to felt, you can use a piece of fabric and

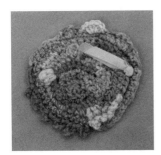

turn the edges under before you sew it down. You might even stiffen it with a little iron-on interfacing. Another possibility is to crochet a plain piece that will fit the bottom of your steeper. It doesn't have to fit exactly.

The fun part isn't over yet. Small additions to your crochet art enliven an already lively project. Add a pompom or a couple of small tassels. Tie on a bit of ribbon, add a charm, sew on a few buttons or a favorite bead.

FURTHER IDEAS

Here are some other ways to encourage the flow of crochet ideas in your creative life:

- Visit a yarn store and let the yarn speak to you. Don't go to make a purchase; just let the ideas come. You might take a small notebook and take the time to record your ideas, focusing on one appealing skein at a time.

  Suggested project: Make a small pillow from yarn you love to support your back in the car or other awkward resting places.

• Play with geometric shapes. Make circles, triangles, rectangles and ellipses. Make your shapes large or small. Sew them together in interesting patterns, even on top of each other.

> *Suggested project*: Make a hot mat of tightly worked, colorful, geometric shapes tacked together.

• Crochet in public. The enthusiasm of curious onlookers will make you feel good about your favorite craft. Interested feedback can inspire your work.

> *Suggested project:* Finger crochet a scarf with bulky weight yarn. Take along an extra ball in case someone asks to try it.

• Download a free pattern from your favorite crochet site. Choose something simple that is worked in a heavy yarn. After you have worked a sample, make up the same pattern in a finer yarn and play with embellishments.

> *Suggested project:* A simple hat worked in double crochets in the round works well for this project. Add flowers, buttons, ribbons, and/or the crocheted doodads of your choosing.

• Purchase a new crochet periodical from the newsstand. While you are there, look at quilting, beading, knitting, and scrapbooking magazines. Color and pattern ideas are everywhere.

> *Suggested project:* Keep a notebook of project ideas and visual design ideas. Make color copies or cut out pictures of anything that inspires you visually. Take photographs yourself. Photographs from nature can inspire new texture and color combinations.

10
The Blessings of Hands
An Appreciation of the Hand that Holds the Hook

MITTENS WITH MEANING

I wonder, did my great-grandmother think about her own hands when she knitted mittens for her great-grandchildren every year? Was she aware of how, as she knitted, she looped herself closer to us and to our hands? Did she think about how important a job her Christmas mittens would perform in the cold upstate New York winters? How delicate were those she entrusted to the mittens' safe-keeping? My great-grandmother, my mother's grandmother, lived to be nearly 106 years old. She made a new pair of mittens every year for each of her great-grandchildren while we were growing up.

Grandma Sutton's mittens were not glamorous. They were always made of plain wool yarn in a solid color: white, green, blue, or an inexpensive ombré. They were not fancy. There were no patterns or textures knitted in. And they were never a surprise. There was nothing to learn from squeezing and shaking our packages except that they held a fresh pair of mittens. Yet I now have a reverence for hands that began to work its way, unwittingly, into my soul with every new pair of mittens, wrapped in festive paper and placed under the Christmas tree.

I have learned the value of my own hands. They are capable of caressing loved ones, feeding a family, tending a house, playing music, sewing clothing, spinning, weaving, knitting, and crocheting. I can now warm someone else's cold hands with colorful, textured crocheted mittens, or cover cold ears with a soft, protective hat using the simplest of tools as extensions of my hands.

I am fascinated with hands. It is with our hands that we come to explore the world, to produce great art, to heal not just ourselves but also creatures of other species. Italian educator and physician Dr. Maria Montessori expressed the importance of our hands when she said, "The truth is that when a free spirit exists, it aches to materialize itself in some form of work, and for this the hands are needed."

In an essay titled "The Hand and the Tool," from a book titled *A Way of Working*, Michael Donner wrote a wonderful paragraph on the spiritual dimension of craft:

> I take a fresh look at my hand and am perhaps astonished this time at the very sight of it. It is an awesome thing—mine and not mine. Among other things, I notice that its structure is uncommitted; it is not frozen into a specialized form such as a hoof or a paw but is free enough—as well as sensitive and intelligent enough—to take up any number of tools and perform highly varied and exacting tasks. A marvelous entity, its very existence calls for the master craftsman to appear, to occupy it, and to give it direction. It is from the emptiness of this hand that a miracle could pass to leave its imprint on matter.

The hand that leaves "its imprint on matter" may, by extension, leave its imprint on soul. This speaks to the impression that Grandma Sutton's handmade mittens made on me. But this fragment of my tale isn't over until I tell you one more detail. With her last hand-warming gift to me, Grandma Sutton quietly, without a word, celebrated my coming of age, a milestone of maturity and new responsibilities to come. The Christmas of my senior year in high school, the colorful Christmas wrapping paper contained not a pair of mittens but a pair of finely wrought, fawn-colored gloves.

THE STAGE IS SET

As I write this, I am expecting my first grandchild. The baby has been growing inside my daughter's body for four months now. Today I learned that two months ago this child-to-be had every necessary part in place in his or her tiny hands. By eight weeks gestation, every bone is in place, at least in the form of cartilage. Some nerves extend to the tips of the fingers. Muscle groups are present, and the hollows of the joints have formed. Every finger is free and independent at the end of the first two months.

This information is even more amazing when we realize that each hand is made up of twenty-seven bones. There are eight irregular pebbly looking bones in each of our wrists. Each of our fingers, including each thumb, has a long metacarpal bone encased within the fleshy main of our hands. The thumb has two phalanx bones, and the other four fingers have three apiece. A three-dimensional weaving of muscles, tendons, and nerves, coupled with articulated bones that glide against each other in a perfect combination of freedom and control, enables our spirits to create. The physical foundations for every hand skill we need to crochet are present at birth.

My grandson, Liam, explores the world through his hands.

I slow myself to observe my own hands as I start to crochet. My eyes connect with what my hands are doing. My left hand pulls the outside end of a ball of yarn toward me. With my thumb and first two fingers, I hold the yarn, leaving about six inches dangling. With my right hand, I twist the end of the yarn to form a loop, then, with my left hand, I secure the crossing. Now I release my hold on the loop to poke my right thumb and first finger through the loop to grab the supply end of the yarn. I pull it back through the loop while maintaining a grasp on the tail end of the yarn with my left hand. I have made a slipknot, the first step in any crochet endeavor.

The beginnings of what will later be sophisticated eye-hand coordinations originate in our first year of life, when we discover our hands. Our eyes behold our small fists waving about, first one, then the other, then both. Our hands become our first playthings as we watch and wiggle our fingers in the air, open and close them, move them closer to our eyes or farther away.

We own a grasp from birth, at first only a reflex, that develops into a will-directed clutch-and-release sequence over the course of our first year. Each of my hands performed at least one such grasp-and-release sequence in the making of my slipknot.

Now I transfer my slipknot to my hook. Hand-to-hand transfer begins around the middle of our first year, and my transfer of the slipknot to the hook held in my other hand is simply a more developed version of that early skill.

When I take the hook in my right hand, I use a knife hold. My first three fingers, working together, oppose my thumb, holding the hook between them. I'm moving along now, making a pretty pink chain, and the finger pads of my left hand are performing a quick grasp-release sequence as I continue to steady the lengthening chain. My right hand grasps the hook and sends it under the yarn supply to grab the yarn and pull it through the previous loop again and again.

All of our basic "grasps" are usually in place by the end of our first year, with our crowning achievement being the superior pincer grasp. This is the grasp I use at the end of my project to pick up the tapestry needle with the tips of my fingers on one hand, then twist, loop, and hold the yarn end to wiggle it through the eye of the needle with the tips of my fingers on the other hand. The beginnings, but only the beginnings, of the full range of future possibilities are accomplished in an explosion of movement while we are still babies. As long as we are given plenty of freedom and encouragement to exercise our hands, they will provide us with much of what we need to apply ourselves to life's necessary work and to express ourselves creatively.

DEEPER DEVELOPMENT

Dr. Frank Wilson, neurologist and medical director of the Peter F. Ostwald Health Program for Performing Artists at the University of California School of Medicine, tells the story of a much older developmental phase of the hand. He begins with a reminder of the well-publicized anthropological find of the hominid named Lucy, who is believed to have lived 3.5 million years ago. Her bone structure puts her in the gray area between apes and humans, and she remains a very important link in our understanding of our past.

Though Lucy was small and chimplike, with a small brain cavity, she walked upright. And her hands, though not fully human, were not exactly those of an ape either. There were exciting modifications in both her hands and wrists. American anthropologist Mary Marzke has studied Lucy's hands and found that Lucy had a longer thumb in relation to her fingers, and that her index finger and middle finger could swivel. The significance of this adaptation is that she was able to form a new grasp that apes did not have. This new hand, coupled with the appropriate shoulder movements, would have enabled Lucy to throw rocks overhand, which could have lead to an important survival strategy. But Dr. Wilson believes that Lucy lacked the structures in her brain to properly time her release so that her projectile would hit a target.

The ability of an ancient being to throw rocks may seem pretty disconnected from what we need to know about crocheting, but if Wilson's theory is true, the two skills may have a very similar effect. His theory is that hand development may have come first, before brain development. This means that our hands might inform or train our brains! Wilson writes, "For the hominids, the small changes in wrist and hand structure led to significantly improved throwing and eventually to a complete reorganization of the brain." Between the time that Lucy lived and the time our hands came to be configured as they are today (100,000 to 200,000 years), our brains tripled in size, we designed more and more complex tools, and we came to live in more civilized and structured communities. This process has not come to a stop. It still goes on today.

When we develop the abilities of our hands, we are developing our intelligence! Every new crochet skill we add builds dendritic connections in our brains. When we crochet and meet the challenges we hold in our hands, we are also likely building our potential to approach any other problem creatively.

Perhaps the most interesting difference between Lucy's hands and ours is that we have ulnar opposition. We hear the phrase "the opposable thumb" fairly often, but the fully modern humans we are today did not develop this until we acquired the ability for the other side of our hand to move toward our palm—an "opposable pinkie." In crocheting, ulnar opposition comes into play more strongly when we use the knife position to hold our hook than it does when we employ the pencil position. Once we developed ulnar opposition, our hands could shape themselves to countless objects and control them in different ways.

Over time, we gained the ability to take objects apart and put them back together again to make entirely new objects. For every connection and reconnection in our hands, our brains continue to gain more ability to connect and reconnect. As Dr. Wilson so succinctly put it, "The brain does not live inside the head, even though that is its formal habitat. It reaches out to the body, and with the body, it reaches out to the world. Brain is hand and hand is brain."

THE HEART CONNECTION

Dr. Maria Montessori, founder of the Montessori educational method, and Rudolph Steiner, founder of the Waldorf educational method, both believed strongly that the freedom to move about is important for developing children, and that activities that incorporate fine motor movements should be part of the training of mind, body, and spirit. Montessori designed a range of beautiful and well-made materials that draw children through basic academic processes under the guidance of a classroom teacher who gives a short lesson on how to manipulate each material. Steiner, who was invited to start a school for the children of workers in a German factory, put a program in place that would strengthen children's hands and incorporate their minds and spirits by focusing on the arts in general and handwork in particular.

In Steiner mixed-age kindergartens, children help prepare their own snacks, garden, bake bread, do simple sewing, and loop finger chains with thick yarn. The children are taught knitting in first grade, before they write, to help strengthen their hands; most children are not ready to knit before then.* In second grade, along with their academic work, music, and art, the children are taught to crochet!

Crochet presents a new challenge because it requires more concentration. Each hand is doing something different. One hand has most of the responsibility for holding up the weight of the project and steadying the work for the other hand. The hook hand moves in and out, twisting slightly and sometimes lifting upward to draw loops through loops. "The balance is different [from knitting] although both hands are busy," says Patricia Livingston, coauthor of *Will-Developed Intelligence: Handwork and Practical Arts in the Waldorf School.*

Livingston has her students make a crocheted potholder as one of their starter projects, knowing that the children will likely give them as gifts to their mothers and will think about the recipients of their gifts as they make them. "The anticipation of pleasing someone cultivates altruism."

It is easy to teach beginning knitters to make stripes, but when the children start to crochet, a new world of color opens up. The children easily make geometric shapes with concentric colors and two-color spirals that look tricky but aren't. It is equally easy to create log cabin-type patterns because each stitch is picked up one at a time and worked before going on to the next one. Toy animals and people appear, constructed of tube shapes crocheted in continuous rounds. The children learn to make useful items, all the while

*Children in Steiner (Waldorf) Schools start first grade academics and learn knitting when they are seven years old. Most children are not ready to knit before then and crochets awaits another year's development.

developing the muscles in their hands, their ability to work, their minds, their artistic sensibilities, and their sensitivity to people. The hand-brain connection becomes a hand-heart connection.

Arvia MacKaye Ege, a poet and longtime Waldorf teacher, summed up the beauty of the hand this way: "An organ of the sense of touch, it can be used to feel, to grasp, to move, mold, intertwine or to relate other objects to one another, but also to make free gestures expressive of the inner dictates of the soul. Through infinite variations of all these, it has become one of [our] most creative and, at the same time, selfless organs."

The first time I read Ege's words, I stopped, just ... stopped. We live in such an information-based culture that we have become head oriented in a way that is out of balance with our hearts. Our minds are always busy. Our hands are always busy. But how often do we stop to meditate on our *heart's* connection to our hands? It is through our hands that our inner spirit, that intimate, deep expression of Spirit, pours into our work and reaches out to the world.

SOUL-FULL HANDS

Artists have often tried to capture—on paper, in clay, and in photographs—what Ege described as "free gestures, expressive of the inner dictates of the soul." Leonardo da Vinci's sketch of one hand cradling another; the *Praying Hands* by Albrecht Dürer; *The Cathedral*, a sculpture of hands by Rodin—all are expressions from the artist's own sensitive hands, bringing a universal understanding of the hands as an expression of the whole self: body, mind, spirit.

Hands may be the most perfect expression of Creation and Creator.

In a small book called *Praying with Our Hands: 21 Practices of Embodied Prayer from the World's Spiritual Traditions* (SkyLight Paths), Jon Sweeney writes, "When words don't adequately say what we mean, our hands might be able to show it." I think that is part of why I crochet. The colors of creation are so beautiful, warmth so important, our bodies so precious as to decorate, the visual balance in our world so soothing, that I need to convey my appreciation through my hands and share it with others. Crochet is one of the ways I express "the inner dictates" of my soul.

Praying with Our Hands captures, with words and photographs, gestures from religious traditions, many of which have their counterparts in everyday life. Pages that speak of the spirituality of work, breaking bread, and showing kindness to others are bound alongside the lighting of Sabbath candles, praying with beads, a mudra from the yogic tradition, the sign of the cross from Catholicism, and the earthward and heavenward gestures of the Sufi dervish. Common gestures become sacred gestures when mindfulness of the sacred is present.

Rev. Billy Graham once said, "The most eloquent prayer is the prayer through hands that heal and bless." In many religious traditions, hand gestures play a central role as expressions of reverence, blessing, and petition.

Open Hands

Perhaps one of the oldest postures for prayer, called the *orans* position (which comes from the Latin word for "praying"), is one of standing with raised open hands. *Orans* means "one who prays" in Latin and is represented 153 times by pictures in the Roman catacombs. *Orans* is a common gesture in Eastern churches, Jewish synagogues, and many Western churches.

Folded Hands

 Folding hands in prayer is a ubiquitous hand gesture found in Christianity, Hinduism, Buddhism, and religions of Tibet and Japan. In India, this gesture goes hand-in-hand with the word *namaste*, which translates as "I bow to the divinity within you from the divinity within me." In the practice of yoga, it is thought that bringing hands together brings the left and right hemispheres of the brain together and calms the mind.

Mudras

In Hinduism and Buddhism, mudras (from a Sanskrit word meaning "seal") are an important part of religious practice. There are hundreds of these symbolic hand gestures, and each has a specific meaning. Mudras have been practiced throughout history, and we have evidence dating as far back as 1500 BCE that hands were used in religious expression: the Egyptian deity Ra was shown as a sunburst with each ray terminating in an open hand. In Islamic mysticism, hand gestures are often used to help produce an altered state of awareness. Sufi dervishes pose their hands in specific mudralike signs while dancing, and some Sufi sects trace the ninety-nine names of God on their bodies with their right hand while engaging in *zikir,* or focusing upon God through chanting.

The Sign of the Cross

The sign of the cross is a ritual hand motion that many Catholics use to trace the shape of the cross in the air or on the body. The sign can be made by individuals as a form of prayer, or by clergy as an act of blessing. The hand sign known as the Christogram is considered the original sign of the cross, and this form of mudra can be seen in many Renaissance paintings and murals of Jesus, the saints, and priests. Today, this sign of benediction—made by extending the thumb and first two fingers and folding the ring and little fingers onto the palms to form the Greek letters *ICXC* (the Greek name for Christ)—is used mainly by priests in the Eastern Orthodox Church. A similar gesture is known in Hindu and Buddhist traditions as the *prana* mudra, a symbol of healing.

Aaronic Blessing

This hand gesture is an ancient Jewish custom that accompanies the *Birkat Kohanim*, or "Priestly Blessing." The blessing is made by spreading the hands into two V shapes, in the form of the Hebrew letter *shin*, and it symbolizes the light of the *Shekhina*, or Presence of God.

Hamsa, Hand of Fatima

The *Hamsa*, or "Hamesh hand," is an ancient symbol used as a protective amulet by both Jews and Muslims. The name *hamsa* comes from the Semitic root meaning "five," and in Jewish use it is sometimes called the Hand of Miriam, after the biblical heroine.

Called the Hand of Fatima by Muslims, this hand sign is named for the daughter of Muhammad, and is sometimes said to symbolize the Five Pillars, or tenets, of Islam.

Heart in Hand

The symbol of a heart in an open palm, called Heart in Hand, is an image that originated with the Shakers and is often found on crafts, signs, and even cookies. The symbol is a pictorial reminder of the words of Mother Ann Lee, the founder of the Shaker sect: "Put your hands to work, and your hearts to God."

Healing Hand

The image of a healing hand, from Native American solar pictographs, is found in many places in the southwestern United States, and its solar spiral most likely represents a shaman's powers. Today, it is often used to symbolize the energy in the healing hands of a Reiki healer.

Handshake

In many liturgical churches, as well as my Friends' meeting, parishioners greet each other with a handclasp or handshake during worship. In some churches, this act is called "passing the peace," and it may also include a greeting and a hug. My meeting is small enough that, often, we all shake hands with everyone else and then chuckle at ourselves, as we make sure we have greeted every last person. The everyday handshake becomes a spiritual greeting and an expression of love for our fellow travelers in the Spirit.

PRACTICING LOVINGKINDNESS FOR HANDS

Our hands, capable of doing so much for us and for others, sometimes tire. Just as the rest of our body can get worn down, so can our hands. They deserve attention, rest, a good stretch, a little affection. In the same way that we would not want to take our loved ones for granted, it is important that we not take our hands for granted. We can show our hands lovingkindness.

It is especially important to be aware of your hands as you crochet. Stretch your hands a bit before you begin. The hook hand usually needs to be stretched more than the supply hand, but you can give your supply hand a stretch also—to keep it from getting jealous.

Mindfulness—keeping yourself aware of how your hands are feeling—is the key to treating your hands lovingly. As you crochet, be compassionately aware of your hands. If your hands or wrist muscles begin to feel taut from the repetitive motion, stop and do a few more simple stretches:

- Place your working hand out before you, palm down and flat, as though you were resting it on a table. Reach with your fingers. Your little finger and thumb are stretching in opposite directions. Spread the middle three fingers. You should feel a good stretch in your fingers, palm, and wrist. Relax your hand. Repeat as is comfortable.

- Another good, gentle stretch is to place your palms together in front of you with your fingers together and pointing up. Now raise your elbows slowly so that your forearms are parallel to the floor. Don't push too hard. You should feel this stretch all the way through the underside of your forearms.

You might also want to give your hands a loving massage. A massage will not only relieve the tension in your hands, but will also help to relax your whole body. You don't have to go to a spa or wait for someone else to be willing to help you treat your hands to this luxury. The simplest of hand massages is to stroke the back of one hand with the palm of the other, moving from the fingertips across the hand and up the arm. You can rest your hand on your stomach to support your fingers. If you like, you can use a little massage oil for this. You might even like to keep several small bottles of aromatic oil just for the purpose. After you complete each side, rest a moment and let the relaxing feeling settle in. For a longer massage, follow these steps:

- Rub a little oil onto the hand that is being massaged (optional).

- Stroke the back of the hand with the palm of the working hand, as you did for the simple massage above. While the palm of the hand being worked on is still facing down, turn the working hand up and massage the fingers from underneath. Gently squeeze each finger, top and bottom, then side to side, working from the fingertips toward the palm.

- Rub gently between the bones on the back of the hand with the thumb of the working hand.

- Now turn the receiving hand over and, keeping the working hand palm-up, support the receiving hand while alternately squeezing the flesh on the palm gently and rubbing it in small circular motions.

- End by turning the receiving hand over and stroking it as you did to start the massage.

If you find your hands are getting sore often or getting very sore, consider giving them some time off. Use them for activities that are different from the ones you have been doing—or go all out and give them a vacation!

You may be familiar with the idea of foot washing, either historically as a sign of hospitality or spiritually as a sign of humility. I'd like to propose that we, as crocheters, consider hand washing.

If you belong to a group that crochets for charity or performs other hand-intensive ministries, you might consider reverently washing and drying each other's hands. You could incorporate hand massage along with the washing. (If the gathering is to include working with fibers, it's better to use a small amount of lotion rather than oil.) This exercise would be especially meaningful with beautiful hand-thrown bowls and hand-woven towels.

In the introduction to *Praying with Our Hands,* Sweeney suggests that we "consciously practice praying with our hands" by holding our hands, open, before us, as a gesture of invitation, acceptance of divine aid, and a symbol of our gift of work back to the Creator. This short, simple, prayerful gesture is appropriate for the crochet work we do and will have the added benefit of reminding us of what treasures our hands are.

THE BLESSINGS OF HANDS QUERIES

What handmade presents did you receive as a child? Did any of them move you or contribute to who you are today?

Have you ever had the experience of watching a child learn to use her hands? What observations did you make? Consider taking some time to observe the next time you are in the company of a baby or a young child.

Consider how your hands are a connection to your heart. How do you feel when you make something to give to another person? When someone gives you something handmade?

Are you mindful of your own hands and all they do? Do you ever stop to watch what your hands are actually doing in the exacting act of crocheting? Give yourself some time to be especially aware of the gift of your hands.

What part do hands play in your spiritual life or that of your faith community?

What might you do to treat your hands reverently?

Lovingkindness Wristers

This project is a wonderful way to treat your hands kindly. Wristers were used a great deal, historically, to warm busy hands in less well-heated homes than ours. Even though your hands are probably not *actually* cold, it is good to warm your working hand and wrist muscles, just as dancers warm their legs. Warm wristers can support the muscles and blood vessels at the base of your hands. So make a pair of Lovingkindness Wristers for yourself, and then make more to warm the hands of all your hard-working friends.

INTENTION

To make a tangible sign of caring for your hands.

MATERIALS

- about 110 yards of worsted weight yarn (I used Bazic Wool from Classic Elite yarns.)
- size H hook (I used a Susan Bates hook.)
- yarn needle
- scissors

Gauge: body of wrister without trim equals 6 inches long, one single crochet row and one double crochet row combined equals ⅞-inch

DIRECTIONS

Wristers

Chain 23.

Row 1: Skip 2 chains and single crochet in the third chain from the hook, single crochet in each chain across the row, turn (21 stitches).

Row 2: Chain 3 (chain does not count as a stitch), double crochet in the first single crochet of the row below and in each stitch across (21 stitches). This is a right side row. Mark it with a stitch marker, pin, or paper clip or just remember that you are working on the right side when the starting tail is on your right. Turn.

Row 3: Chain 1 (chain does not count as a stitch), single crochet in the first double crochet of the row below, single crochet in each stitch across, turn (21 stitches).

Row 4: Chain 3, double crochet in the next stitch and in each stitch across, turn (21 stitches).

Row 5: Chain 1, single crochet in the next stitch and in each stitch across including the turning chain, turn.

Repeat rows 4 and 5 six more times (15 rows total).

Last row: Chain 3, 1 double crochet in each of the next 9 stitches, 1 half double crochet in each of the next 2 stitches, 1 single crochet in each of the next 3 stitches, 1 half double crochet in each of the next 2 stitches, and 1 double crochet in the remaining 5 stitches, turn.

Check for size: If your wristers are too tight, you can use longer stitches in the last row, or take out the last row and add another repeat consisting of a row of double crochet and a row of single crochet. If your wrister is too large, you can try taking out a repeat.

Joining the Edges

Fold your wrister so that the starting edge and the ending edge are aligned and the right side is on the inside. Chain 1. Inserting the hook under both loops of the stitches in the ending row and two loops of the starting chains, slip stitch the two edges together including the edges of the chain loops at the end of the row. End off, thread in the ends.

Scallops

Make a slip knot and place it on your hook. Insert the hook into the edge *opposite* the 3-chain turning chain loops and next to the seam. Make one slip stitch. Insert the hook into the edge of the single

Close-up of scallops.

crochet row to the left of the seam and make five half double crochets. Slip stitch in the edge of the next double crochet row. Continue around making five half double crochets in each single crochet row edge and a slip stitch in the edge of each double crochet row. Make a scallop in the last single crochet row and slip stitch in the same space as the first slip stitch. End off. Thread in the ends. Now make one for the other hand.

FURTHER IDEAS

• For an extra feminine touch, thread a length of ribbon through the chained loops at the back of your wristers.

• These wrist warmers may also serve a man who works in the cold but needs his fingers free. Leave off the row of scallops at the finger end and, instead, add a row of basic stitches.

• Think about making a pair of wristers for an older person or someone with arthritis. The offer of a hand massage as a gift along with your crocheted warmers may be a long-cherished blessing.

• Make a pair of Lovingkindness Wristers as a special gift for a crocheter or knitter friend.

A Concluding Letter

Dear Reader,

As I was writing this book, I often thought of you and wondered who you might be. I have tried throughout to leave open spaces for you and your thoughts. I have put forward ideas but tried not to draw too many conclusions. Much of that will be for you to do. While I have kept you in mind and encouraged you to continue the conversation, I also hope you have found places in your life where your crochet can contribute beauty and comfort to others. I have shared a broad range of spiritual ideas, many of my favorites from my faith community, along with gleanings from religions and cultures other than my own. I have offered my understandings of craft as a spiritual endeavor. Along the way, I have met many others who understand how art and craft become spiritual practices, and I have made new knitting and crochet friends. I fervently hope that the blessings I have been given will bless you and your crochet projects. Thank you for your presence.

CINDY CRANDALL-FRAZIER
End Off!

Acknowledgments

I am grateful to the women who contributed to this book by sharing with me their love of crochet and their thoughts about the spiritual connections to our craft. Thanks, also, to my friends and family, crocheters and noncrocheters alike, who read or listened patiently to my rough drafts and made helpful comments.

Three editors played a part in bringing this book to fruition, each of them wise and skilled in her own way. Maura Shaw trusted the process when she invited me to write a book about crochet and spirituality. Emily Wichland supported me through the initial creation of the manuscript. And Marcia Broucek had the most difficult job, that of spinning flax into gold. I am grateful for the caring work of each.

I am also grateful to acknowledge the following people for their contributions: Heather Cox, for her thoughts on freeform mandalas; Melody MacDuffee, for her thoughts on the spiritual dimensions of crochet; Gail Conklin, for her thoughts on crochet as healing; Karen Klemp, for her ideas on yarn storage; Jane Brown, owner of Craftique/Never Enough Knitting shop in Wheaton, Illinois, for her help in crocheting samples for the project directions.

Finally, grateful thanks to my husband, Richard, for his ability to see through the camera's eye and for giving me the support I need to "follow my bliss."

Suggestions for Further Reading

Alexander, Scott W. *Everyday Spiritual Practices: Simple Pathways for Enriching Your Life*. Boston: Skinner House Books, 2001.

Arguelles, Jose, and Miriam Arguelles. *Mandala*. Boston: Shambhala, 1995.

Auer, Arthur. "Hand Movements Sculpt Intelligence," in *Learning about the World through Modeling-Sculptural Ideas for School and Home*, edited by David Mitchell. Boulder, Colo.: AWSNA Publications, 2001.

Barber, Elizabeth Wayland. *Women's Work: The First 20,000 Years: Women, Cloth, and Society in Early Times*. New York: W. W. Norton, 1995.

Burton, Michael Hedley. *In the Light of a Child: A Journey through the 52 Weeks of the Year in Both Hemispheres for Children and for the Child in Each Human Being* Great. Barrington, Mass.: SteinerBooks, 1998.

Cameron, Julia. *The Artist's Way: A Spiritual Path to Higher Creativity*. Los Angeles: Jeremy P. Tarcher, 1992.

Campbell, Joseph, and Bill Moyers. *The Power of Myth*. New York: Anchor Books, 1991.

Cornell, Judith. *Mandala: Luminous Symbols for Healing*. 10th ann. ed. Wheaton, Ill.: Quest Books, 2006.

Crandall-Frazier, Cindy. *Single Crochet for Beginners*. Iola, Wis.: Krause Publications, 2005.

———. *Sock Doll Workshop: 30 Delightful Dolls to Create and Cherish*. New York: Lark Books, 2005.

Cunningham, Bailey. *Mandala: Journey to the Center*. New York: DK Publishing, 2002.

Dass, Baba Ram (Richard Alpert). *Be Here Now*. New York: Crown, 1971.

Davis, Jane. *Felted Crochet*. Iola, Wis.: Krause Publications, 2005.

Doczi, Gyorgy. *The Power of Limits: Proportional Harmonies in Nature, Art, and Architecture*. Boston: Shambhala, 2005.

Donner, Michael. "The Hand and the Tool." In *A Way of Working: The Spiritual Dimension of Craft*, edited by E. M. Dooling. New York: Parabola Books, 1986.

Eaton, Jan. *200 Crochet Blocks for Blankets, Throws and Afghans: Crochet Squares to Mix and Match*. Loveland, Colo.: Interweave Press, 2004.

Elgin, Duane. *Voluntary Simplicity: Toward a Way of Life That Is Outwardly Simple, Inwardly Rich*. Rev. ed. New York: Quill, 1998.

Fincher, Susanne F. *Creating Mandalas: For Insight, Healing and Self-Expression*. Boston: Shambhala, 1991.

Fox, Matthew. *Creativity: Where the Divine and the Human Meet*. New York: Jeremy P. Tarcher, 2002.

Gibran, Kahlil. *The Prophet*. New York: Knopf, 1995.

Hanh, Thich Nhat. *The Long Road Turns to Joy: A Guide to Walking Meditation*. Berkeley, Calif.: Parallax Press, 1996.

Henry, Gray, and Susannah Marriott. *Beads of Faith: Pathways to Meditation and Spirituality Using Rosaries, Prayer Beads, and Sacred Words*. Louisville: Fons Vitae, 2008.

Johnson, Wendy. "On Gardening: Arranging Garbage," in *Tricycle: The Buddhist Review* 16, no. 2 (2006).

Jorgensen, Susan S., and Susan S. Izard. *Knitting into the Mystery: A Guide to the Shawl-Knitting Ministry*. New York: Morehouse, 2003.

Lambert, Patricia, Barbara Staepelaere, and Mary G. Fry. *Color and Fiber*. Atglen, Pa.: Schiffer Books, 1986.

MacDuffee, Melody. *Overlay Crochet Jewelry*. Little Rock, Ark.: Leisure Arts, 2006.

Mitchell, David S. and Patricia Livingston. *Will-Developed Intelligence: Handiwork and the Practical Arts in the Waldorf Schools*. Boulder, Colo.: AWSNA Publications, 1999.

Morrow, Susan, and Mark Dittrick. *Contemporary Crochet*. New York: Lancer Books, 1972.

Mountford, Debra, ed. *The Harmony Guide to Crocheting: Techniques and Stitches*. New York: Harmony Books, 1992.

Murphy, Bernadette. *Zen and the Art of Knitting: Exploring the Links between Knitting, Spirituality, and Creativity.* Avon, Mass.: Adams Media, 2002.

Norton, Carol. *Tapestry Crochet.* Loveland, Colo.: Interweave Press, 1991.

Pagoldh, Susanne. *Nordic Knitting: Thirty-one Patterns in the Scandinavian Tradition.* Loveland, Colo.: Interweave Press, 1997.

Palmer, Parker J. *Let Your Life Speak: Listening for the Voice of Vocation.* San Francisco: Jossey-Bass, 2000.

Paludan, Lis. *Crochet: A History and Technique.* Loveland, Colo.: Interweave Press, 1995.

Searle, Teresa. *Heartfelt: 25 Projects for Stitched and Felted Accessories.* New York: St. Martin's Griffin, 2006.

Skolnik, Linda, and Janice MacDaniels. *The Knitting Way: A Guide to Spiritual Self-Discovery.* Woodstock, Vt.: SkyLight Paths, 2005.

Smith, Robert Lawrence. *A Quaker Book of Wisdom: Life Lessons in Simplicity, Service and Common Sense.* New York: Harper Paperbacks, 1999.

Spurkland, Kristin. *Crochet from the Heart: Quick Projects for Generous Giving.* Woodinville, Wash.: Martingale, 2005.

Stearns, Ann. *Batsford Book of Crochet.* London: B.T. Batsford, 1987.

Steiner, Rudolf. *Calendar of the Soul: The Year Participated.* Translated by Owen Barfield. London: Rudolf Steiner Press, 2006.

Stephenson, Susan. *The Joyful Child: For Birth to Three Years.* Michael Olaf's Essential Montessori Series. Arcata, Calif.: Michael Olaf Montessori, 1998.

Sweeney, Jon M. *Praying with Our Hands: 21 Practices of Embodied Prayer from the World's Spiritual Traditions.* Woodstock, Vt.: SkyLight Paths, 2000.

Ventura, Carol. *Beaded and Felted Tapestry Crochet.* Cookeville, Tenn.: Carol Ventura, 2006.

———. *More Tapestry Crochet.* Cookeville, Tenn.: Carol Ventura, 2002.

Wiley, Eleanor, and Maggie Oman Shannon. *A String and a Prayer: How to Make and Use Prayer Beads.* Boston: Red Wheel/Weiser, 2002.

Wilson, Frank R. *The Hand: How Its Use Shapes the Brain, Language, and Human Culture.* New York: Vintage, 1999.

———. "The Real Meaning of Hands-On Education," in *Research Bulletin: The Research Institute for Waldorf Education* 5, no. 1 (2000).

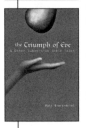

Children's Spirituality

ENDORSED BY CATHOLIC, PROTESTANT, JEWISH, AND BUDDHIST RELIGIOUS LEADERS

Remembering My Grandparent: A Kid's Own Grief Workbook in the Christian Tradition *by Nechama Liss-Levinson, PhD, and Rev. Molly Phinney Baskette, MDiv* 8 x 10, 48 pp, 2-color text, HC, 978-1-59473-212-6 **$16.99** *For ages 7 & up*

Does God Ever Sleep? *by Joan Sauro, CSJ*
A charming nighttime reminder that God is always present in our lives.
10 x 8½, 32 pp, Full-color photos, Quality PB, 978-1-59473-110-5 **$8.99** *For ages 3–6*

Does God Forgive Me? *by August Gold; Full-color photos by Diane Hardy Waller*
Gently shows how God forgives all that we do if we are truly sorry.
10 x 8½, 32 pp, Full-color photos, Quality PB, 978-1-59473-142-6 **$8.99** *For ages 3–6*

God Said Amen *by Sandy Eisenberg Sasso; Full-color illus. by Avi Katz*
A warm and inspiring tale that shows us that we need only reach out to each other to find the answers to our prayers.
9 x 12, 32 pp, Full-color illus., HC, 978-1-58023-080-3 **$16.95**
For ages 4 & up (A book from Jewish Lights, SkyLight Paths' sister imprint)

How Does God Listen? *by Kay Lindahl; Full-color photos by Cynthia Maloney*
How do we know when God is listening to us? Children will find the answers to these questions as they engage their senses while the story unfolds, learning how God listens in the wind, waves, clouds, hot chocolate, perfume, our tears and our laughter.
10 x 8½, 32 pp, Full-color photos, Quality PB, 978-1-59473-084-9 **$8.99** *For ages 3–6*

In God's Hands *by Lawrence Kushner and Gary Schmidt; Full-color illus. by Matthew J. Baek*
9 x 12, 32 pp, Full-color illus., HC, 978-1-58023-224-1 **$16.99** *For ages 5 & up (A book from Jewish Lights, SkyLight Paths' sister imprint)*

In God's Name *by Sandy Eisenberg Sasso; Full-color illus. by Phoebe Stone*
Like an ancient myth in its poetic text and vibrant illustrations, this award-winning modern fable about the search for God's name celebrates the diversity and, at the same time, the unity of all the people of the world.
9 x 12, 32 pp, Full-color illus., HC, 978-1-879045-26-2 **$16.99**
For ages 4 & up (A book from Jewish Lights, SkyLight Paths' sister imprint)

Also available in Spanish: **El nombre de Dios**
9 x 12, 32 pp, Full-color illus., HC, 978-1-893361-63-8 **$16.95**

In Our Image: God's First Creatures
by Nancy Sohn Swartz; Full-color illus. by Melanie Hall
A playful new twist on the Genesis story—from the perspective of the animals. Celebrates the interconnectedness of nature and the harmony of all living things.
9 x 12, 32 pp, Full-color illus., HC, 978-1-879045-99-6 **$16.95**
For ages 4 & up (A book from Jewish Lights, SkyLight Paths' sister imprint)

Noah's Wife: The Story of Naamah
by Sandy Eisenberg Sasso; Full-color illus. by Bethanne Andersen
This new story, based on an ancient text, opens readers' religious imaginations to new ideas about the well-known story of the Flood. When God tells Noah to bring the animals of the world onto the ark, God also calls on Naamah, Noah's wife, to save each plant on Earth.
9 x 12, 32 pp, Full-color illus., HC, 978-1-58023-134-3 **$16.95**
For ages 4 & up (A book from Jewish Lights, SkyLight Paths' sister imprint)

Also available: **Naamah:** Noah's Wife (A Board Book)
by Sandy Eisenberg Sasso; Full-color illus. by Bethanne Andersen
5 x 5, 24 pp, Full-color illus., Board Book, 978-1-893361-56-0 **$7.99** *For ages 0–4*

Where Does God Live? *by August Gold and Matthew J. Perlman*
Helps children and their parents find God in the world around us with simple, practical examples children can relate to.
10 x 8½, 32 pp, Full-color photos, Quality PB, 978-1-893361-39-3 **$8.99** *For ages 3–6*

Spirituality of the Seasons

Autumn: A Spiritual Biography of the Season
Edited by Gary Schmidt and Susan M. Felch; Illustrations by Mary Azarian
Rejoice in autumn as a time of preparation and reflection. Includes Wendell Berry, David James Duncan, Robert Frost, A. Bartlett Giamatti, E. B. White, P. D. James, Julian of Norwich, Garret Keizer, Tracy Kidder, Anne Lamott, May Sarton.
6 x 9, 320 pp, 5 b/w illus., Quality PB, 978-1-59473-118-1 **$18.99**

Spring: A Spiritual Biography of the Season
Edited by Gary Schmidt and Susan M. Felch; Illustrations by Mary Azarian
Explore the gentle unfurling of spring and reflect on how nature celebrates rebirth and renewal. Includes Jane Kenyon, Lucy Larcom, Harry Thurston, Nathaniel Hawthorne, Noel Perrin, Annie Dillard, Martha Ballard, Barbara Kingsolver, Dorothy Wordsworth, Donald Hall, David Brill, Lionel Basney, Isak Dinesen, Paul Laurence Dunbar. 6 x 9, 352 pp, 6 b/w illus., Quality PB, 978-1-59473-246-1 **$18.99**

Summer: A Spiritual Biography of the Season
Edited by Gary Schmidt and Susan M. Felch; Illustrations by Barry Moser
"A sumptuous banquet.... These selections lift up an exquisite wholeness found within an everyday sophistication." — ★ *Publishers Weekly* starred review
Includes Anne Lamott, Luci Shaw, Ray Bradbury, Richard Selzer, Thomas Lynch, Walt Whitman, Carl Sandburg, Sherman Alexie, Madeleine L'Engle, Jamaica Kincaid.
6 x 9, 304 pp, 5 b/w illus., Quality PB, 978-1-59473-183-9 **$18.99**
HC, 978-1-59473-083-2 **$21.99**

Winter: A Spiritual Biography of the Season
Edited by Gary Schmidt and Susan M. Felch; Illustrations by Barry Moser
"This outstanding anthology features top-flight nature and spirituality writers on the fierce, inexorable season of winter.... Remarkably lively and warm, despite the icy subject." — ★ *Publishers Weekly* starred review
Includes Will Campbell, Rachel Carson, Annie Dillard, Donald Hall, Ron Hansen, Jane Kenyon, Jamaica Kincaid, Barry Lopez, Kathleen Norris, John Updike, E. B. White.
6 x 9, 288 pp, 6 b/w illus., Deluxe PB w/ flaps, 978-1-893361-92-8 **$18.95**

Spirituality / Animal Companions

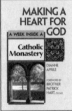

Blessing the Animals: Prayers and Ceremonies to Celebrate God's Creatures, Wild and Tame *Edited and with Introductions by Lynn L. Caruso*
5¼ x 7¼, 256 pp, Quality PB, 978-1-59473-253-9 **$15.99**; HC, 978-1-59473-145-7 **$19.99**

Remembering My Pet: A Kid's Own Spiritual Workbook for When a Pet Dies
by Nechama Liss-Levinson, PhD, and Rev. Molly Phinney Baskette, MDiv; Foreword by Lynn L. Caruso
8 x 10, 48 pp, 2-color text, HC, 978-1-59473-221-8 **$16.99**

What Animals Can Teach Us about Spirituality: Inspiring Lessons from Wild and Tame Creatures *by Diana L. Guerrero* 6 x 9, 176 pp, Quality PB, 978-1-893361-84-3 **$16.95**

Spirituality—A Week Inside

Come and Sit: A Week Inside Meditation Centers
by Marcia Z. Nelson; Foreword by Wayne Teasdale
6 x 9, 224 pp, b/w photos, Quality PB, 978-1-893361-35-5 **$16.95**

Lighting the Lamp of Wisdom: A Week Inside a Yoga Ashram
by John Ittner; Foreword by Dr. David Frawley
6 x 9, 192 pp, 10+ b/w photos, Quality PB, 978-1-893361-52-2 **$15.95**

Making a Heart for God: A Week Inside a Catholic Monastery
by Dianne Aprile; Foreword by Brother Patrick Hart, OCSO
6 x 9, 224 pp, b/w photos, Quality PB, 978-1-893361-49-2 **$16.95**

Waking Up: A Week Inside a Zen Monastery
by Jack Maguire; Foreword by John Daido Loori, Roshi
6 x 9, 224 pp, b/w photos, Quality PB, 978-1-893361-55-3 **$16.95**; HC, 978-1-893361-13-3 **$21.95**

Spiritual Practice

Laugh Your Way to Grace: Reclaiming the Spiritual Power of Humor
by Rev. Susan Sparks A powerful, humorous case for laughter as a spiritual, healing path. 6 x 9, 144 pp (est), Quality PB, 978-1-59473-280-5 **$16.99**

Haiku—The Sacred Art: A Spiritual Practice in Three Lines
by Margaret D. McGee Introduces haiku as a simple and effective way of tapping into the sacred moments that permeate everyday living.
5½ x 8½, 192 pp, Quality PB, 978-1-59473-269-0 **$16.99**

Dance—The Sacred Art: The Joy of Movement as a Spiritual Practice
by Cynthia Winton-Henry Invites all of us, regardless of experience, into the possibility of dance/movement as a spiritual practice.
5½ x 8½, 224 pp, Quality PB, 978-1-59473-268-3 **$16.99**

Spiritual Adventures in the Snow: Skiing & Snowboarding as Renewal for Your Soul *by Dr. Marcia McFee and Rev. Karen Foster; Foreword by Paul Arthur* Explores snow sports as tangible experiences of the spiritual essence of our bodies and the earth. 5½ x 8½, 208 pp, Quality PB, 978-1-59473-270-6 **$16.99**

Recovery—The Sacred Art: The Twelve Steps as Spiritual Practice
by Rami Shapiro; Foreword by Joan Borysenko, PhD Uniquely interprets the Twelve Steps of Alcoholics Anonymous to speak to everyone seeking a freer and more God-centered life. 5½ x 8½, 240 pp, Quality PB, 978-1-59473-259-1 **$16.99**

Everyday Herbs in Spiritual Life: A Guide to Many Practices
by Michael J. Caduto; Foreword by Rosemary Gladstar
7 x 9, 208 pp, 20+ b/w illus., Quality PB, 978-1-59473-174-7 **$16.99**

Divining the Body: Reclaim the Holiness of Your Physical Self *by Jan Phillips*
8 x 8, 256 pp, Quality PB, 978-1-59473-080-1 **$16.99**

The Gospel of Thomas: A Guidebook for Spiritual Practice
by Ron Miller; Translations by Stevan Davies 6 x 9, 160 pp, Quality PB, 978-1-59473-047-4 **$14.99**

Hospitality—The Sacred Art: Discovering the Hidden Spiritual Power of Invitation and Welcome *by Rev. Nanette Sawyer; Foreword by Rev. Dirk Ficca*
5½ x 8½, 208 pp, Quality PB, 978-1-59473-228-7 **$16.99**

Labyrinths from the Outside In: Walking to Spiritual Insight—A Beginner's Guide
by Donna Schaper and Carole Ann Camp
6 x 9, 208 pp, b/w illus. and photos, Quality PB, 978-1-893361-18-8 **$16.95**

Practicing the Sacred Art of Listening: A Guide to Enrich Your Relationships and Kindle Your Spiritual Life *by Kay Lindahl* 8 x 8, 176 pp, Quality PB, 978-1-893361-85-0 **$16.95**

Running—The Sacred Art: Preparing to Practice *by Dr. Warren A. Kay; Foreword by Kristin Armstrong* 5½ x 8½, 160 pp, Quality PB, 978-1-59473-227-0 **$16.99**

The Sacred Art of Bowing: Preparing to Practice
by Andi Young 5½ x 8½, 128 pp, b/w illus., Quality PB, 978-1-893361-82-9 **$14.95**

The Sacred Art of Chant: Preparing to Practice
by Ana Hernández 5½ x 8½, 192 pp, Quality PB, 978-1-59473-036-8 **$15.99**

The Sacred Art of Fasting: Preparing to Practice
by Thomas Ryan, CSP 5½ x 8½, 192 pp, Quality PB, 978-1-59473-078-8 **$15.99**

The Sacred Art of Forgiveness: Forgiving Ourselves and Others through God's Grace
by Marcia Ford 8 x 8, 176 pp, Quality PB, 978-1-59473-175-4 **$16.99**

The Sacred Art of Listening: Forty Reflections for Cultivating a Spiritual Practice
by Kay Lindahl; Illustrations by Amy Schnapper 8 x 8, 160 pp, b/w illus., Quality PB, 978-1-893361-44-7 **$16.99**

The Sacred Art of Lovingkindness: Preparing to Practice
by Rabbi Rami Shapiro; Foreword by Marcia Ford 5½ x 8½, 176 pp, Quality PB, 978-1-59473-151-8 **$16.99**

Sacred Speech: A Practical Guide for Keeping Spirit in Your Speech
by Rev. Donna Schaper 6 x 9, 176 pp, Quality PB, 978-1-59473-068-9 **$15.99**
HC, 978-1-893361-74-4 **$21.95**

Soul Fire: Accessing Your Creativity
by Thomas Ryan, CSP 6 x 9, 160 pp, Quality PB, 978-1-59473-243-0 **$16.99**

Thanking & Blessing—The Sacred Art: Spiritual Vitality through Gratefulness
by Jay Marshall, PhD; Foreword by Philip Gulley 5½ x 8½, 176 pp, Quality PB, 978-1-59473-231-7 **$16.99**

Spirituality & Crafts

Beading—The Creative Spirit: Finding Your Sacred Center through the Art of Beadwork *by Rev. Wendy Ellsworth*
Invites you on a spiritual pilgrimage into the kaleidoscope world of glass and color.   7 x 9, 240 pp, 8-page color insert, 40+ b/w photos and 40 diagrams
Quality PB, 978-1-59473-267-6 **$18.99**

Contemplative Crochet: A Hands-On Guide for Interlocking Faith and Craft *by Cindy Crandall-Frazier; Foreword by Linda Skolnik*
Illuminates the spiritual lessons you can learn through crocheting.
7 x 9, 208 pp, b/w photos, Quality PB, 978-1-59473-238-6 **$16.99**

The Knitting Way: A Guide to Spiritual Self-Discovery
by Linda Skolnik and Janice MacDaniels Examines how you can explore and strengthen your spiritual life through knitting.
7 x 9, 240 pp, b/w photos, Quality PB, 978-1-59473-079-5 **$16.99**

The Painting Path: Embodying Spiritual Discovery through Yoga, Brush and Color *by Linda Novick; Foreword by Richard Segalman*
Explores the divine connection you can experience through art.
7 x 9, 208 pp, 8-page color insert, plus b/w photos
Quality PB, 978-1-59473-226-3 **$18.99**

The Quilting Path: A Guide to Spiritual Discovery through Fabric, Thread and Kabbalah *by Louise Silk*
Explores how to cultivate personal growth through quilt making.
7 x 9, 192 pp, b/w photos and illus., Quality PB, 978-1-59473-206-5 **$16.99**

The Scrapbooking Journey: A Hands-On Guide to Spiritual Discovery
by Cory Richardson-Lauve; Foreword by Stacy Julian   Reveals how this craft can become a practice used to deepen and shape your life.
7 x 9, 176 pp, 8-page color insert, plus b/w photos, Quality PB, 978-1-59473-216-4 **$18.99**

The Soulwork of Clay: A Hands-On Approach to Spirituality
by Marjory Zoet Bankson; Photos by Peter Bankson
Takes you through the seven-step process of making clay into a pot, drawing parallels at each stage to the process of spiritual growth.
7 x 9, 192 pp, b/w photos, Quality PB, 978-1-59473-249-2 **$16.99**

Kabbalah / Enneagram
(Books from Jewish Lights Publishing, SkyLight Paths' sister imprint)

God in Your Body: Kabbalah, Mindfulness and Embodied Spiritual Practice
by Jay Michaelson 6 x 9, 272 pp, Quality PB, 978-1-58023-304-0 **$18.99**

Cast in God's Image: Discover Your Personality Type Using the Enneagram and Kabbalah
by Rabbi Howard A. Addison 7 x 9, 176 pp, Quality PB, 978-1-58023-124-4 **$16.95**

Ehyeh: A Kabbalah for Tomorrow *by Dr. Arthur Green*
6 x 9, 224 pp, Quality PB, 978-1-58023-213-5 **$16.99**

The Enneagram and Kabbalah, 2nd Edition: Reading Your Soul
by Rabbi Howard A. Addison 6 x 9, 192 pp, Quality PB, 978-1-58023-229-6 **$16.99**

The Gift of Kabbalah: Discovering the Secrets of Heaven, Renewing Your Life on Earth
by Tamar Frankiel, PhD 6 x 9, 256 pp, Quality PB, 978-1-58023-141-1 **$16.95**

Kabbalah: A Brief Introduction for Christians
by Tamar Frankiel, PhD 5½ x 8½, 176 pp, Quality PB, 978-1-58023-303-3 **$16.99**

Zohar: Annotated & Explained *Translation & Annotation by Daniel C. Matt*
Foreword by Andrew Harvey 5½ x 8½, 176 pp, Quality PB, 978-1-893361-51-5 **$15.99**

Spirituality

Creative Aging: Rethinking Retirement and Non-Retirement in a Changing World   *by Marjory Zoet Bankson*
Offers creative ways to nourish our calling and discover meaning and purpose in our older years.   6 x 9, 160 pp, Quality PB, 978-1-59473-281-2 **$16.99**

Laugh Your Way to Grace: Reclaiming the Spiritual Power of Humor
by Rev. Susan Sparks   A powerful, humorous case for laughter as a spiritual, healing path.   6 x 9, 144 pp (est), Quality PB, 978-1-59473-280-5 **$16.99**

Living into Hope: A Call to Spiritual Action for Such a Time as This
by Rev. Dr. Joan Brown Campbell; Foreword by Karen Armstrong
A visionary minister speaks out on the pressing issues that face us today, offering inspiration and challenge.   6 x 9, 192 pp (est), HC, 978-1-59473-283-6 **$21.99**

Claiming Earth as Common Ground: The Ecological Crisis through the Lens of Faith   *by Andrea Cohen-Kiener; Foreword by Rev. Sally Bingham*
Inspires us to work across denominational lines in order to fulfill our sacred imperative to care for God's creation. 6 x 9, 192 pp, Quality PB, 978-1-59473-261-4 **$16.99**

The Losses of Our Lives: The Sacred Gifts of Renewal in Everyday Loss
by Dr. Nancy Copeland-Payton
Reframes loss from the perspective that our everyday losses help us learn what we need to handle the major losses. 6 x 9, 192 pp, HC, 978-1-59473-271-3 **$19.99**

Bread, Body, Spirit: Finding the Sacred in Food
Edited and with Introductions by Alice Peck   6 x 9, 224 pp, Quality PB, 978-1-59473-242-3 **$19.99**

Creating a Spiritual Retirement: A Guide to the Unseen Possibilities in Our Lives
by Molly Srode   6 x 9, 208 pp, b/w photos, Quality PB, 978-1-59473-050-4 **$14.99**

Finding Hope: Cultivating God's Gift of a Hopeful Spirit
by Marcia Ford; Foreword by Andrea Jaeger   8 x 8, 176 pp, Quality PB, 978-1-59473-211-9 **$16.99**

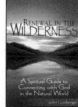

Honoring Motherhood: Prayers, Ceremonies and Blessings
Edited and with Introductions by Lynn L. Caruso   5 x 7¼, 272 pp, HC, 978-1-59473-239-3 **$19.99**

Jewish Spirituality: A Brief Introduction for Christians   *by Lawrence Kushner*
5½ x 8½, 112 pp, Quality PB, 978-1-58023-150-3 **$12.95** *(A book from Jewish Lights, SkyLight Paths' sister imprint)*

Journeys of Simplicity: Traveling Light with Thomas Merton, Bashō, Edward Abbey, Annie Dillard & Others   *by Philip Harnden*
5 x 7¼, 144 pp, Quality PB, 978-1-59473-181-5 **$12.99**; 128 pp, HC, 978-1-893361-76-8 **$16.95**

Keeping Spiritual Balance As We Grow Older: More than 65 Creative Ways to Use Purpose, Prayer, and the Power of Spirit to Build a Meaningful Retirement
by Molly and Bernie Srode   8 x 8, 224 pp, Quality PB, 978-1-59473-042-9 **$16.99**

Money and the Way of Wisdom: Insights from the Book of Proverbs
by Timothy J. Sandoval, PhD   6 x 9, 192 pp, Quality PB, 978-1-59473-245-4 **$16.99**

Next to Godliness: Finding the Sacred in Housekeeping
Edited by Alice Peck   6 x 9, 224 pp, Quality PB, 978-1-59473-214-0 **$19.99**

Renewal in the Wilderness
A Spiritual Guide to Connecting with God in the Natural World
by John Lionberger   6 x 9, 176 pp, b/w photos, Quality PB, 978-1-59473-219-5 **$16.99**

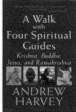

Soul Fire: Accessing Your Creativity
by Thomas Ryan, CSP   6 x 9, 160 pp, Quality PB, 978-1-59473-243-0 **$16.99**

A Spirituality for Brokenness: Discovering Your Deepest Self in Difficult Times
by Terry Taylor   6 x 9, 176 pp, Quality PB, 978-1-59473-229-4 **$16.99**

Spiritually Incorrect: Finding God in All the *Wrong* Places   *by Dan Wakefield; Illus. by Marian DelVecchio*   5½ x 8½, 192 pp, b/w illus., Quality PB, 978-1-59473-137-2 **$15.99**

A Walk with Four Spiritual Guides: Krishna, Buddha, Jesus, and Ramakrishna
by Andrew Harvey   5½ x 8½, 192 pp, 10 b/w photos & illus., Quality PB, 978-1-59473-138-9 **$15.99**

The Workplace and Spirituality: New Perspectives on Research and Practice
Edited by Dr. Joan Marques, Dr. Satinder Dhiman and Dr. Richard King
6 x 9, 256 pp, HC, 978-1-59473-260-7 **$29.99**

About SKYLIGHT PATHS Publishing

SkyLight Paths Publishing is creating a place where people of different spiritual traditions come together for challenge and inspiration, a place where we can help each other understand the mystery that lies at the heart of our existence.

Through spirituality, our religious beliefs are increasingly becoming a part of our lives—rather than *apart* from our lives. While many of us may be more interested than ever in spiritual growth, we may be less firmly planted in traditional religion. Yet, we do want to deepen our relationship to the sacred, to learn from our own as well as from other faith traditions, and to practice in new ways.

SkyLight Paths sees both believers and seekers as a community that increasingly transcends traditional boundaries of religion and denomination—people wanting to learn from each other, *walking together, finding the way.*

For your information and convenience, at the back of this book we have provided a list of other SkyLight Paths books you might find interesting and useful. They cover the following subjects:

Buddhism / Zen	Global Spiritual	Monasticism
Catholicism	Perspectives	Mysticism
Children's Books	Gnosticism	Poetry
Christianity	Hinduism /	Prayer
Comparative	Vedanta	Religious Etiquette
Religion	Inspiration	Retirement
Current Events	Islam / Sufism	Spiritual Biography
Earth-Based	Judaism	Spiritual Direction
Spirituality	Kabbalah	Spirituality
Enneagram	Meditation	Women's Interest
	Midrash Fiction	Worship

Or phone, fax, mail or e-mail to: SKYLIGHT PATHS Publishing
Sunset Farm Offices, Route 4 • P.O. Box 237 • Woodstock, Vermont 05091
Tel: (802) 457-4000 • Fax: (802) 457-4004 • www.skylightpaths.com
Credit card orders: (800) 962-4544 (8:30AM–5:30PM ET Monday–Friday)
Generous discounts on quantity orders. SATISFACTION GUARANTEED. Prices subject to change.

For more information about each book,
visit our website at www.skylightpaths.com